Bluff

Bluff

The Game
Central Banks
Play and
How it Leads
to Crisis

**Anjum
Hoda**

ONEWORLD

A Oneworld Book

First published in North America, Great Britain and
Australia by Oneworld Publications, 2016

ISBN 978-1-78074-813-9
ISBN 978-1-78074-814-6 (eBook)

Text design and typeset by Tetragon, London
Printed and bound in Great Britain by Clays Ltd, St Ives plc

Oneworld Publications
10 Bloomsbury Street
London WC1B 3SR
England

I saw true liberty walking the streets and standing at thresholds begging for refuge, and the people turning her away. Then I saw degradation moving in a great procession, and the people calling it liberty.

The Vision, Kahlil Gibran

Contents

Preface

I t took Joseph Heller seven years to write *Catch-22*; I recall reading that fact at some point growing up and being perplexed at how it could take anyone that long to write a book. Time had yet to shorten; perception changes rapidly as we mature. I first attempted to write this book in 2009, but after about ten months of effort, my enthusiasm ebbed.

Then in autumn 2012, I was invited to a dinner for the great and the good of the firm I worked for. As I took a seat on one of the round tables next to my name tag, a colleague from another division approached to take the place next to me. He looked askance at my name card and threw his hands in the air, exclaiming irritably, 'I just know my career is going nowhere by the person I am seated next to.' I smiled politely and said, 'Likewise.'

Further into the dinner, a Board member struck up a conversation from across the table. As he was speaking, the chatter broke and the others listened in. He said, 'I haven't seen you before, you must have joined recently.' I said, 'Yes, that is correct.'

'So where did you make your career, then?' he continued. I explained and described what I did. To which he replied, 'Ahh, interest rates. You know they're very important to us. What do you think then, can they rise?' referring to rates on US Treasuries.

'Well, if they did, everything else would collapse. I guess they could rise but I reckon only by some market accident rather than central bank intent. Which means that it would be an unmissable opportunity to buy government bonds.'

'So you are worried then, about such an accident?'

'No, not really,' I replied, then grinned and added on a lighter note, 'or perhaps I am, as that's why I don't have a mortgage.'

At which point, the gentleman next to me hissed loudly, 'You see, *bankers!*' Followed by what effectively implied, 'You see, bankers – how they have stolen from a tax-paying public to enrich themselves, so much so that they can afford to buy in London outright!' I was a little taken aback by his lack of grace and regrettably didn't come up with a clever enough response, for nothing could have been further from the truth. As for a mortgage, I simply didn't have one as I rented at that time.

I went home that night thinking of how misunderstood the reasons for the crisis were, my thoughts once more gravitating towards finishing this book. In my near two decades in the financial industry, for sure I saw fear, insecurity and elbowing competitiveness as there can be no complete escape from the human condition. But for the most part, I encountered professionalism and a strong work ethic driven by the motive of profit that lies at the heart of enterprise. What I certainly didn't see were wilful deceit and the intent to cheat.

I didn't start writing in earnest until late in 2013, after having set in motion a chain of events earlier that year that would permit me the freedom to do so. After six months of frenetic writing, I asked someone whose opinion I valued if he could give me his thoughts on my unpolished, first draft. He agreed and told me that the thesis was powerful; then gently relayed that the writing style was a dud. That was enough encouragement for me.

I pressed delete and rewrote. In the meantime, I met Andrew Gordon of David Higham Associates who gave me some tips on the art of narration and book construction that came in handy. I am indebted to Oneworld Publications for publishing this book; to Mike Harpley, its then editorial director, for first picking up on it notwithstanding the fact that its theme ran counter to the commercially more lucrative spin of Wall Street greed and glamour. I am grateful to Ben Sumner – the sting of his editorial comment made for some sharper text.

And last but not least, this book is dedicated to my parents – for the gift of life and for demonstrating the values of hard work and simple living.

December, 2015
London, England

Part I

Introduction

1

The Need to Question

In his 1859 work *On Liberty*, John Stuart Mill wrote:

> In the present age – which has been described as *destitute of faith, but terrified at scepticism* – in which people feel sure, not so much that their opinions are true, as that they should not know what to do without them – the claims of an opinion to be protected from public attack are rested not so much on its truth, as on its importance to society.[1]

Some 150 years on, Mill's words – which describe our unwillingness to question belief structures – are an apt portrayal of our attitude towards central banks. As controllers of money – an economic necessity that serves the twin purposes of medium of exchange and store of value – the central banks have been accorded a position of key importance in society. Their decisions have gone unquestioned mostly because of the indispensability of their role, rather than our conviction of its correctness. We have acquiesced to their ideological prescription that a continual loss of purchasing power facilitated by low interest rates is necessary to create a stable and robust economic future. At the same time, our lack of faith in paper money has goaded us into risky investments. The resulting investment frenzy has led to dazzling gains in real estate, equities, gold and other assets over short periods of time. And a subliminal dread that high public debt gives governments a motive to create yet more inflation has at times only intensified the rush.

Yet, since the late 1990s, while real estate prices and equity markets have shown bursts of exuberance, our incomes have lagged far behind. As a result, rises in the prices of assets have not been built on a firm foundation of proportionally higher incomes. Instead, they have been created and sustained by low interest rates. Consequently, each time interest rates have risen, the values of these investments have crashed, leaving behind a trail of economic woe. Despite the repercussions of the juddering volatility in asset prices, we have come to accept the tax of continual inflation and excessive manoeuvring of interest rates as an effective economic remedy.

Our disinclination to question the central banks' actions stems from fear – fear that the equity, bond and real estate markets are no longer a reflection of the wealth of our society but instead a leviathan that threatens it. The incentive to chase house prices and bet in equity markets is very strong, especially when set against weak job prospects, little power to negotiate wages and the pressure of inflation. But the blinding returns from these investments have a dark side: they end up holding our economic fortunes and livelihoods to ransom. This is why we are terrified of tackling the central banks: once most of us have been suckered in to risky investments, we want their values to keep going higher. So we see no option but to rely on the central banks to continually prop them up with ever lower interest rates.

The currently accepted narrative for the 2007–09 financial collapse is that it was caused by the greed and deceit of commercial and investment bankers and traders. The truth, however, is that even after the financial crisis and the reining in of investment and commercial banks that followed it, real estate prices and financial markets have continued to remain unstable, hurtling upwards, only to violently lurch downwards. This instability betrays the fact that the cause of the financial crisis lies elsewhere.

The business model of commercial banking[2] is premised on the banks' need to hold only a fraction of customers' deposits to fund cash withdrawals. They then lend the rest to businesses and individuals over long periods, or equivalently invest in debt securities issued by various borrowers to raise funds. This activity allows the banks to earn higher returns than they pay their depositors. The model is similar to the one employed by gyms, which offer memberships to far more people than they can accommodate at any one time. Gym owners assume that not all their members will turn up at the same time to use the facilities – otherwise they would have a problem. Similarly, bankers assume that not all their customers will withdraw their cash at the same time, thereby ensuring that there are large sums of money deposited over long periods.

However, by making risky investments for longer periods while nonetheless enabling customers to withdraw their money at any time, commercial banks are exceptionally vulnerable to an extraordinary increase in demand for cash. Faced with this demand, they are forced to call in their loans and sell their assets.

This inevitably precipitates business closures, job losses and a fall in prices – not only of risky debt securities, but also real estate (as it is usually bought on credit) and shares (as they are claims of ownership of publicly traded companies).

Such a situation can quickly spiral downwards: as all banks try to raise cash, the likelihood of recession and financial loss increases. As a result, banks and investors refrain from making risky investments, which only worsens the downturn and reinforces their reluctance. To prevent a self-perpetuating downspin of financial panic and recession, it falls to the central banks (as independent arms of government) – the Bank of England and the US Federal Reserve in the context of this book – to intervene as lenders of last resort. As loans and debt securities are essentially promises made by borrowers to pay fixed sums of money in the future, they can be converted into cash by deducting the interest that is payable between now and the due date. The central banks therefore stabilise[3] the financial system by offering cash in lieu of these discountable investments, deducting interest or discounting[4] them at the prevailing rate.

Before the central banks took on this stabilising role, it was not uncommon for mistrust in banks to spark financial panics. The Walt Disney classic *Mary Poppins*, set in London in the early 1900s, contains an excellent, if simplistic, depiction of such contagion. George Banks, a prosperous officer at the Fidelity Fiduciary Bank in the City of London, takes his young children Jane and Michael on a trip to his workplace. As he introduces them to his bosses, Mr Dawes Senior, the elderly chairman of the bank, takes Michael's pocket money out of his hand while trying to impress upon him the prudence of investing it. Uninspired by the prospect of financing 'railways through Africa and dams

6

across the Nile', Michael decides he would rather use his allowance to buy bird feed. As he yells to have his tuppence back, he unwittingly triggers a run on the Fidelity Fiduciary – hearing his panicked cries, other customers start withdrawing their cash en masse, mistakenly fearing that the bank is unable to pay out.

Mary Poppins is set in an Edwardian London at the zenith of British imperial and financial power, but the scene reflects a tale more familiar on the other side of the Atlantic. After the Civil War, the US economy had been plagued by recurring banking crises. In 1873, 1884, 1890, 1893 and 1907, individual bank failures caused by economic slowdowns fuelled widespread fear of further failures. This fear led to runs on otherwise solvent banks, causing them to fail. In the ensuing scramble for cash, banks then halted customer withdrawals, further exacerbating the panic. To shore up cash, the banks were also forced to restrict lending to businesses and households, creating a credit shortage (or 'crunch' as it is more popularly referred to nowadays) that turned slowdowns into nastier, more damaging recessions.

The banking panic of 1907 had so severe an impact on the economy that the need for monetary reform could no longer be ignored. It precipitated the eventual creation of the US Federal Reserve system, in December 1913. The Fed's main purpose was to 'furnish an elastic currency' in the form of the Federal Reserve note – giving it the power to quickly create large sums of money and then to reduce it when it was no longer needed (hence the term 'elastic'). This allowed the US Federal Reserve to come to the aid of a banking system in need of liquidity or cash to satisfy customers clamouring at the gates for their money. By being able to borrow from the Fed, banks no longer had to restrict their lending or customer cash withdrawals, and the overall level of credit in the economy stayed stable despite a short-term spike in demand for liquidity.

Bank failures were a major exacerbating cause of the economic malaise of 1929–33 in the US, referred to as the Great Depression. The contraction of credit and distressed sales of assets by banks in the want for cash set in motion a downspin of falling prices, business closures and debt defaults that further compounded the stress in the banking system. Given the circumstance of its birth, it was unsurprising that the Federal Reserve was later judged by politicians and economic historians as not having done enough to aid the banking system and the economy.

The slur of not having done enough was not forgotten, not least by its more recent leaders Ben Bernanke and his predecessor Alan Greenspan. Nevertheless, in September 2008, against a febrile economic backdrop of heavy debt – in both the financial sector and many millions of US households – events transpired to create a situation in which investment bank Lehman Brothers was allowed to go under. Despite that miscalculation, however, the US Federal Reserve did subsequently save the financial system from collapse by exercising the 'lender of last resort' role its elastic currency had originally intended it to have. However, even though the Fed saved the economy, ironically it was also largely responsible for sowing the seeds of the global financial crisis that first began in 2007 with defaults by sub-prime mortgage borrowers in the US and culminated in an acute crisis of confidence after the collapse of Lehman Brothers.

The ability to expand an elastic currency in the short term gives the Fed the flexibility to act as lender of last resort to a financial institution at all times – a feature shared by the Bank of England. However, the power to alter the price of money (the rate of interest we earn on our savings and pay as the cost for borrowing), and create inflation at the same time, allows the central banks to affect growth and employment. To understand the culpability of the central banks, we have to separate their role as lender of last resort from their key function of creating maximum growth and employment.

The game the central banks play in running the economy is predicated on a bluff: that by lowering interest rates they can propel the public into economic activity that leads to greater prosperity characterised by more jobs and wages. At the outset, investors are lured into risky financial investments such as stocks, corporate bonds and real estate by cheaper borrowing costs and the promise of higher wages that will ultimately provide the buying power to sustain these asset prices. At the same time, an inadequate return on savings in interest-earning bank accounts or via risk-free investments in government securities in the face of inflation gives investors a further prod to invest in risky assets. The thrall of the apparent wealth created by a rush to invest generates a tremendous 'feel-good' factor, but it does not necessarily serve as a conduit for higher wages. In the absence of higher wages, asset prices and higher levels of indebtedness can be sustained only by lower and lower risk-free interest rates, and the illusion that greater prosperity is just around the corner. Both of these factors act to continually make risky investments attractive. The downside is that these assets then become vulnerable to investors' changing perceptions, as well as any appreciable rise in the cost of borrowing.

The central banks' bluff may well lead to higher wages such that asset prices are not at the mercy of low interest rates. But it was a failed bluff on the part of the central banks that caused the financial crisis of 2007–09. The fact that bankers, investors and traders made good money in the short-term boom facilitated by the central banks allowed for the perfect cover-up. It enabled the central bankers to pin the blame for the economic casualties on them, when a game they orchestrated ran amok.

2

The Motive for the Bluff

The Free Dictionary[1] gives three definitions of the verb *to bluff*: '1. To mislead or deceive; 2. To impress or deter or intimidate by a false display of confidence; 3. To try to deceive opponents in a card game by heavy betting on a poor hand or by little or no betting on a good one.'

The suggestion that the central banks '*mislead and impress the public with a false display of confidence*' may appear not only unseemly but also without obvious motive. How can an institution with the power to alter the price of money and provide unlimited liquidity so lack assurance in its ability to affect economic outcomes that it needs to mislead the public?

The answer lies in the old proverb 'You can lead a horse to water but you cannot make it drink.' The central banks can lower the cost of borrowing, but there is no guarantee that the public will respond accordingly. The motive for the central bankers' bluff becomes clearer when we consider the 'prisoners' dilemma' as a way to think about people's reaction to lower interest rates. In essence, people's fear that others may not act to their advantage makes them susceptible to choosing an inferior outcome.

The 'prisoner's dilemma' describes the predicament faced by two people who have been arrested and are being held in solitary confinement on suspicion of a crime they are guilty of. But the prosecutor does not have the requisite proof: the prisoners can only be convicted of a minor charge. So each prisoner is offered a deal: if he testifies that the other committed the crime, he goes free while the other is convicted and receives a harsh sentence. What follows is that if they then both choose to testify against one another, they end up serving a long sentence which is only slightly mitigated on account of their co-operation. The best outcome for both prisoners is therefore to stay silent and get away with only minor reprimands. However, because each man fears that the other may betray him both testify to take advantage of the prosecutor's deal. Instead of trusting one another and staying silent, they rationally choose an inferior outcome, and serve much longer jail terms than they need have.

Imagine now that there is widespread unemployment and one in five people who wish to work cannot find jobs. To alleviate the situation, the central bank lowers interest rates in the hope that businesses will be encouraged to borrow money, to buy more equipment and hire more people to produce more goods and services. But will that necessarily happen? Consider a shoe manufacturer who is already in debt. A lower rate of interest may lighten his debt service burden, increasing his profits on existing sales. However, before he can invest in more tools and staff to make more shoes – as the central bank intends – he needs to be confident that more people have jobs and/or higher incomes in the first place; or at least that they will be more likely to spend a greater portion of their money. A toymaker thinks the same: if other businesses hire more people, those people will have more money to spend, and she can invest in making more toys. And so on.

Clearly it is in everyone's interest to hire more staff: if more people are earning, more money is being spent on goods and services, creating more profits for businesses. However, businesses are likely to fret that others will not follow suit if they expand. If spending members of the public are unsure about the availability of jobs, they in turn will spend less. As businesses and consumers continue to doubt each other's intentions, fewer people find work: not only do people earn less overall but also individually, because surplus labour keeps wages low. Just like the prisoners, members of the public end up choosing an outcome that leaves them less well off than if they had trusted one another. For cheap money to spur growth, people must overcome their doubt and trust in one another's ability and willingness to earn and spend money.

It is because of this doubt and mistrust that lowering interest rates does not suffice in itself as a strategy for growth. It is the reason why central banks must display a confidence – a certain swagger – backed up, if need be, by coercive tactics to demonstrate that they can compel the public to spend. They may start by presuming that the public will respond positively to a reduction in the cost of borrowing, because lower interest payments give people more to spend. Soon enough, however, the central banks have to lower the interest rate below that of inflation – effectively taxing our savings, as any return we get is no longer enough to compensate for the loss of purchasing power caused by inflation. If that doesn't work, the intimidation gets more blatant: the central banks promise that they won't raise rates for a long time. Here they believe that a protracted loss of purchasing power will be enough to goad even the thriftiest of scrooges to spend, and the most risk-averse to invest.

The promise of low interest rates for a long while carries a risk: that individuals and businesses will take on more debt than is prudent. However, any note of caution from the central banks could prove self-defeating at this stage, and a lacklustre attempt to goad an increasingly doubtful public may prove fatal. So on the central banks go, trying to create economic momentum by intimidating people with a continued reduction in purchasing power, even if this misleads people into more debt. Moreover, no sooner has the public fallen for the bluff and started to borrow, spend and invest with gusto – believing that interest rates will remain low for some time – then there begins an uncomfortable rise in prices. It soon becomes clear that the central banks will have to backtrack from their promise, assuming, of course, that they are serious about keeping the pace of inflation under control. And what about those who thought it was okay to pile on debt because rates were going to be low for a long time? Central bankers, although they are aware that it may be painful for some who took them at their word, assume that on the whole a rising tide will eventually generate higher incomes to compensate for a higher cost of borrowing.

The central banks' bluff is rooted in the paradox of thrift: as one person's spending is another's income, if we are *all* thrifty, we will *all* end up poorer rather than richer. Inadequate spending and investment because of excessive thrift or doubt leads to unemployment and a lower level of overall prosperity. So the central banks resort to their bluff in an attempt to alter mass psychology.

If the suggestion that the central bank is a deceitful and manipulative arm of government feels a little sinister, think of it instead as a strict parent: the mother or father who, keen to get their children to bed by 8pm, warns them of the big, bad bogey-man who comes knocking on the door past bedtime, eager to take naughty children away to a land with no sweets. As central bankers will tell you, their deception and gentle intimidation are laced with the best of intentions – in this case helping the economy to realise its full potential.

Historically, the roles of the Bank of England and the US Federal Reserve were shaped by the need for smooth and easy access to credit, the vicissitudes of prices, and banking panics. The need for a benevolent warden with a special interest in psychological conditioning was more of a post-Second World War imperative: a product of Keynesian economics premised on the paradox of thrift. It was a role that the Federal Reserve would come to play to its full extent only under the leadership of Alan Greenspan in 1987. Since then, the heft of the central banks has soared alongside the multi-dimensionality of their task list. However, rather than benefiting from a new era of economic calm, we have instead seen a dramatic rerun of most of the crises that spurred the entire evolution of central banking over the past three centuries.

3

From Mere Mortal
to Supreme Being

Up until 1640 in England, the primary role of a bank as a parking place for the public's money was fulfilled by the Royal Mint, then housed in the Tower of London. It was here that trusting merchants deposited their surplus coin and bullion for safe-keeping. However, a reservoir of public wealth within arm's length of a king convinced of his divine right to rule was always going to be at risk. In the run-up to the English Civil War between the Parliamentarians and the Royalists, King Charles I was keen to secure funds to maintain a standing army as a mark of his dominance – a stance not favoured by Parliament, which was determined to block his demand for monies for such a purpose. In desperation, he raided the Royal Mint of £130,000 worth of gold bullion, an act that deeply shocked and angered the merchants. Though the bullion was eventually returned, the merchants' confidence in the Royal Mint as a place of safe custody was irreparably damaged. In response, they resorted to entrusting their money to their clerks and cashiers, but after the outbreak of civil war in 1642, many of those people fled, taking their employers' monies with them. The merchants eventually turned to the goldsmiths as they had the requisite knowledge of precious metals and money-changing. At a time when the Royal Mint was no longer deemed safe, these goldsmiths emerged as more trustworthy custodians.[1]

It was customary for them to issue receipts against the coin and bullion that they accepted for safe-keeping. These receipts were no more than written promises to pay back the monies deposited with them. It soon transpired that members of the public were happy to leave their wealth with the goldsmiths for long periods, who could then use these deposits to discount bills of exchange[2] that arose from commercial transactions and offer loans to earn interest. What had started out as a safe custody facility thus turned into the deposit-taking and lending model of fractional reserve banking, wherein banks hold only a part of their customers' deposits and use the rest to earn a higher return (than what they pay to their customers).

The credit facility freed merchants from having to hold idle capital to cover any cash shortfall that arose from a timing mismatch between sale receipts and payments; the goldsmith bankers provided the requisite liquidity by discounting their bills of exchange for cash. Commerce thus acquired more scale, which was further helped by the convenience of paper receipts versus its more bulky metallic counterpart.

With the profits that they acquired from these activities, the goldsmith bankers soon started to pay interest on the deposits, to encourage people to leave their spare monies with them. As their popularity grew and more capital gravitated towards them, they were able to allow their depositors to withdraw money without notice. The facility of credit, the convenience of paper money and ease of access of money made the goldsmith receipts ever more acceptable – so much so that they began to circulate more than coins and were to act as predecessors of modern bank notes.

Eventually even the government came looking for loans, attracted by the large pools of capital the goldsmiths had accumulated. Oliver Cromwell, reluctant to ask Parliament to levy more taxes to pay for a large army, was the first to resort to loans from the goldsmith bankers during the Interregnum under his rule after the end of the English Civil War. After the restoration of the monarchy in 1660, Charles II continued to use the goldsmith bankers for loans that were ultimately backed by taxes. A system was established whereby the public deposited savings with the goldsmith bankers who then lent it to the government at a much higher rate of interest than was paid to depositors.

Although the Church's prohibition of usury had been formalised by royal edict in the 1300s, these laws were repealed in 1495, implicitly allowing lenders to charge interest. In 1545 Henry VIII legalised the charging of interest, setting a limit of 10 per cent, which was reduced to 8 per cent in 1624 and then to 6 per cent in 1651. However, these limits were not adhered to, as the loan rates charged by the goldsmith bankers were much higher. At first they charged the government 8 per cent while paying their depositors 6 per cent. But as the king's demands for loans increased, so did the bankers' rates – to 12 per cent and higher, at times as much as 20 or 30 per cent (the rates charged to the public were equally extortionate).

For all the trust invested in the goldsmith bankers, they were not wholly without risk. In the event of the goldsmiths' bankruptcy, depositors had no guarantee that their coined money and bullion would be returned, and they stood to lose all their savings. With time, the need was forcefully felt for a bank that could offer less usurious interest rates and issue and guarantee a paper currency backed by its metallic counterpart to provide the scale and convenience that business required. It was clear that such an entity would necessarily have to be backed by the State, as only it had the wherewithal by the might of taxation to be able to provide for such a guarantee. However, the memory of the king's raid on the Royal Mint triggered fears that a state-backed bank was vulnerable to an expropriation of funds. It was a sentiment that was only reinforced by the events of 1672 when, short of money, Charles II had ordered the suspension of payments from the Exchequer for a period of twelve months. The government owed the goldsmith bankers £1.3 million at the time, so they in turn stopped paying their depositors. This led to widespread bankruptcy and panic among all those who had deposited money with the goldsmith bankers.

It was not until 1694 that a confluence of circumstance made a state-backed national bank possible. Five years into a war with France's Sun King Louis XIV, the British government was once again in considerable need of funds, despite having already squeezed everything it could out of duties and taxes. Britain now had a constitutional monarchy (put in place by the Glorious Revolution of 1688), which made the public more conducive to the idea of a national bank: the separation of the national budget from the king's expenses meant that expropriation of funds was deemed unlikely. The government therefore finally turned to the idea of forming a national bank to secure a loan, and the Bank of England was formed in 1694 by an Act of Parliament.

'The Governor and Company of the Bank of England', as the private corporation was formally called, raised £1.2 million as capital from various shareholders, which was then lent to the government at the rate of 8 per cent interest per annum. The total annual interest charge of £100,000 included a £4,000 fee for the Bank's management and governance, which was to be undertaken by a governor, a deputy governor and twenty-four directors, elected each year from among the shareholders of the company. In return for low-cost loans at below the market rate of interest, the corporation was allowed various banking privileges, which included the permission to issue bank notes by way of discounting bills of exchange or in lieu of the coin and bullion that it took in, much as the goldsmiths had done.

The notes issued by the Bank of England were to be payable in gold or coinage on demand to the bearer of the note. Even though the Bank was not obliged to hold gold and bullion in one-to-one correspondence with the notes it issued, the principles of sound banking required it nonetheless to maintain a large reserve of cash (coins and bank notes) and bullion to meet customer withdrawals. The paper notes it issued acted as a medium of exchange, and as they were spent in the economy, they eventually found their way as deposits into customer bank accounts. If private profit (which arose from the interest deductions made while discounting bills of exchange) led the Bank to issue too many notes, then customers could withdraw more from their bank accounts – either to hold in their pockets as cash or to exchange out in gold to pay for foreign goods. This naturally drained bank reserves, threatening its viability as a bank and acting as an in-built constraint on the number of notes it could issue.

Shortly thereafter in 1697, convertibility of notes issued by the Bank of England to gold was guaranteed by the State such that in the event of non-payment by the bank they could be presented at the Exchequer by the bearer of the note for payment out of the interest due from the government to the bank. Consequently, the quantity of bank notes issued was not to exceed the total capital lent to the government. Importantly, the Bank of England was to be the only state-backed bank. This was vital to reassure the public that other such entities did not compete for government funds against which the notes were ultimately secured. Soon its bank notes came to circulate more freely as they came with a sense of security that the goldsmith bankers were unable to offer for their receipts.

The interest earned on the capital loaned to the government and banking privileges soon led to juicy profits that resulted in large dividend payments to the stakeholders of the Bank of England. During the course of the following century, the pattern that developed was one shaped by mutual benefit. In exchange for an extension of its charter and the opportunity to earn prof-its through banking privileges, the Bank provided further loan capital to the government at progressively lower rates of interest.

In a grant of further favour in return for such additional loans, an Act of Parliament in 1709 bolstered the monopoly of the Bank of England by forbidding other large joint-stock com-panies from issuing notes and conducting banking business in England. Other than the Bank of England, only smaller banks whose shares were held by no more than six persons were allowed to operate. However, this monopoly would soon pose a problem as by construct such banks did not have the deep pockets of the larger players, nor their discipline, and were prone to issuing notes far in excess of their reserves of its metallic counterpart.

As Bank of England notes only circulated in London, the merchants in the provinces were forced to rely upon such smaller banks to discount their bills of exchange for cash in the form of private bank notes. As the economy grew, and trade and commerce flourished across England over the course of the eighteenth century, these smaller country banks grew rapidly in number from just twelve in 1750 to 400 by 1793. They provided credit to the merchants by discounting their bills of exchange and in turn depended on the Bank of England to offer them liquidity against them. This facility to acquire cash against their assets from the Bank of England if and when needed allowed them to get by with low reserves to meet customer withdrawals.

However, a severe economic downturn in 1792 resulted in many bankruptcies and cast doubt on the worth of much of the circulating paper credit. Consequently, in February 1793, the Bank of England refused to offer liquidity to a small country bank; given its inadequate cash reserves, it in turn had to suspend payment of £1 million to meet its liabilities. Its inability to pay caused a series of further bankruptcies and many more country banks failed. Mistrust spread and there were runs even on solvent banks, which were forced to stop payment and contract note issuance to merchants in order to protect themselves. Credit became even scarcer. The Bank of England acted as any other private institution and raised its discount rate and contracted its note issuance to protect itself from losses, effectively compounding the economic distress caused by the shortage of credit.

The crisis continued until the government finally agreed to issue £5 million in Exchequer bills, which were interest-bearing promises to pay on demand, as an alternative paper currency. The merchants were offered these bills against the collateral of their commercial wares. The mere knowledge that credit was available ended the cycle of mistrust and economic contraction. Economic activity recovered and the return of confidence meant that the entire £5 million did not have to be advanced: although the initial request for credit was only for roughly three-quarters of the full amount, the government ultimately advanced even less. In the end, the government made a small profit on the credit it extended and only two borrowers actually went bankrupt. In the absence of a central bank acting as lender of last resort, it was evident that it fell upon the State to restore mercantile confidence for the benefit of the tax-paying public, and doing so indeed made for a win-win situation.

While the Bank of England was still to step up to the role of stabilising the banking system, its role as government financier only increased in importance during its first hundred years. The French Revolutionary Wars began in 1792 and were soon followed by the Napoleonic Wars, which lasted until 1815. Burgeoning expenses would lead William Pitt, then prime minister, to draw excessively upon the Bank of England for financing but the resulting increase in bank notes in circulation inevitably drained bank reserves. So in an attempt to preserve its reserves, by 1796 the Bank had sought to restrict the issuance of notes to the commercial world.

Soon after, however, in early 1797, fears of an imminent French invasion sparked a major panic. Members of the public and country banks alike scrambled to withdraw as much coined money as possible. The Bank's reserves dwindled further and by February 1797 had fallen substantially, leaving it in a position close to bankruptcy – the drain on its reserves due to excessive demand for coined money meant that it would soon be unable to meet the claims of its customers. It was no longer a question of preserving its reserves by restricting its note issuance: it had already done so quite considerably only to have the counterproductive effect of heightening the panic. The absence of paper notes had only increased the demand for coined money as the public sensed restriction of convertibility and sought to withdraw more of it. The nature of the panic left the Bank with little choice. With the counsel of the king and Parliament, the Bank suspended convertibility to gold; a controversial event that would trigger a discourse on the legitimacy of a paper currency that would eventually lead to the full Gold Standard in 1844.

From 1797 to 1821 Britain effectively had a paper currency which was no longer backed by its metallic counterpart and was therefore unconstrained by its physical limits. Pitt, however, had been aware of the possibility of hyperinflation as had happened in France in the case of the French Assignats – the paper currency issued by the government during the French Revolution. He had therefore exercised prudence and had reduced his demands on the Bank of England for money advances and resorted to taxation by introducing income tax to raise revenues. Thus the period from 1797 to 1809 was one of stable prices and money supply, despite Britain having a paper currency without the anchor of convertibility to gold. However, discipline soon gave way to excess as the public became enamoured by the promise of investing in South America. The Bank of England helped fuel the speculative fever with an over-issue of notes, as did the small country banks, which had almost doubled in number since 1793.

The apprehension that a paper currency without the limits imposed by convertibility would prove to be inflationary soon started to be justified. Consumer prices[3] rose sharply in 1809 and 1810 by a total of 12.5 per cent. This rapid rise alongside a falling exchange rate consequently led to a government inquiry – the Bullion Committee of 1810 – which established that these were symptoms caused by an over-issuance of notes. This conclusion gave credence to the view that a currency not bound by the limits of underlying coin and bullion was susceptible to the indiscipline of over-issuance for the sake of private profit at the discretion of its issuers and therefore had no legitimate basis. The argument gained further ground as prices rose by another 16 per cent from 1812 to 1813.

With its legitimacy in question, paper currency was never going to last long once the Napoleonic Wars were over in 1815. Convertibility of paper currency to gold was re-established by 1821, with the inevitable result of a drastic reduction in the quantity of notes in circulation in the economy. Prices soon fell by 32 per cent between 1818 and 1822. However, convertibility boosted confidence considerably and the economy rebounded sharply thereafter. As convertibility did not necessarily preclude over-issue in the short run, the Bank of England together with the smaller country banks lent heavily into the inflationary boom. Prices rose by 36 per cent over the three years to 1825, which gave way to another deflationary phase triggered by a financial crisis centred once again on the smaller country banks.

These large fluctuations in the purchasing power of paper currency led to an increasing preoccupation at the Bank of England with managing its expansion and contraction, in order to achieve stability around the long-term price level dictated by the stock of gold. With this intent, the Bank of England exercised its discretion, relying on a flexible rule to control the amount of paper currency that circulated in the economy. Moreover, the problem of weak country banks was regulated away. An Act of Parliament in 1826 allowed large joint-stock companies to set up banks: lending moved from weak country banks to larger and gradually fewer joint-stock banks. However, the 1830s did not fare better in terms of overall economic stability either. While allowing the joint-stock banks to independently issue notes helped with the problem of weak country banks, the power ceded by the Bank of England soon posed another problem – its own prudence was neutralised by excessive issuance of paper money by the joint-stock banks. Prices rose by 25 per cent between 1835 and 1839. Increased access to credit from the joint-stock banks at lower rates of interest was soon funnelled into speculative investments in the on-going railway boom, paving the way for another deflationary bust.

The instability caused by excessive bank note issuance by the Bank of England and the large joint-stock banks triggered a debate between two schools of thought on the role of money. One stressed the merits of money as a store of value as taking precedence over its function as a medium of exchange. The other stressed its role as a medium of exchange to facilitate business activity. The currency principle, as the former was referred to, argued that paper money in itself had no intrinsic value and was advantageous only on account of the greater efficiency and convenience it permitted versus the use of its metallic counterpart. It was to act solely as a one-to-one substitute for gold, such that these benefits did not come at the cost of an erosion of purchasing power. Its amount had therefore to be regulated and made to conform to the limits imposed by the quantity of its metallic counterpart. This entailed restricting the Bank's discretion in the amount of paper currency it could issue by binding it to the stock of gold and at the same time preventing any superfluous note issuance – as first the small country banks and then the joint-stock banks were seen to have been doing.

The banking principle, on the other hand, did not support any limits on the amount of money in circulation, allowing banks discretion in determining the level of note issuance. So long as notes were convertible to gold and banks operated on sound banking principles which ensured the provision of adequate cash reserves to meet customer withdrawals, it claimed that there could be no over-issuance as lending was determined by the needs of business and commerce. Any superfluous note issuance would therefore only return to the bank unused.

In this 'rules versus discretion' debate, it was rules that eventually won. Further iterative regulation in 1844 granted the Bank sole authority to issue new notes and enshrined the full Gold Standard – linking the quantity of paper currency one-for-one with its monetary gold stock. Private bank notes were to be phased out, such that over time only those issued by the Bank of England came to circulate in the economy.

To ensure that the Bank adhered transparently to the Gold Standard, it was split into two departments. The Issue department was restricted to issuing notes, the quantity of which was secured by up to £14 million in government debt and beyond that fully by coin or bullion. The price of gold was fixed in pounds and the Bank was obliged to buy and sell gold within a fraction of that level.

While the Issue department held the stock of gold to fulfil the convertibility of the paper notes, the Banking department acted like any other bank with assets and liabilities. As per the principle of fractional reserve banking, it was therefore required to hold a part of its assets in the form of a cash reserve, held mostly in notes, to meet the withdrawal needs of its customers. It nonetheless remained different from other banks as among its customers there were not only private individuals and companies, but also country banks, joint-stock banks and clearing houses. It was in this sense a bankers' bank. Importantly, these financial institutions held more than just their account balances at the Banking department – they held their emergency cash reserves there too, reserves that they could call upon to meet the liquidity needs of their own customers.

The limit of fixed issue posed a severe constraint on the Banking department's ability to act as lender of last resort. Its cash reserve was all it could pay out to meet the liquidity needs of its clients. Moreover, as it was made up mostly of bankers' deposits, the entire banking system depended upon it. In the event that there was a sudden panic increase in demand for cash by the entire banking system, it was possible that its cash reserve could prove insufficient. The solution was for it to hold a much larger cash reserve than any of its banking customers. However, holding unused capital had a cost for its shareholders. It was therefore unwilling to do so, even if it was in favour of the stability of the rest of the financial system. Subsequent crises would expose the fault line – the lack of elasticity of cash reserve in times of crisis – imposed by the Act of 1844. Eventually, the State would have to intervene to protect the interests of the commercial world by temporarily suspending the Act each time there was a crisis.

The crisis of 1866 began with the failure of a large, much respected joint-stock discount bank called Overend, Gurney and Company – an episode with parallels to the collapse of Lehman Brothers in 2008. Five years earlier, the suspension of convertibility of the dollar to gold following the outbreak of the American Civil War in 1861 had caused a considerable outflow of gold into Europe. As gold flew into the coffers of the Bank of England, it could issue more paper currency against it. The resulting increase in money supply and fall in interest rates boosted economic activity. On the downside, however, low interest rates led to lax standards in lending and fuelled speculative behaviour in the London money market.

It had been customary in the London money market for banks to lend money at call (at short notice) to discount houses and bill brokers, against the collateral of bills of exchange. The usual practice – to lend money at call against the security of a bill of exchange – ensured that the credit quality of the asset (bill of exchange, in this case) against which the loan was made was demonstrably sound. As it came to pass, however, the larger discount houses were allowed leeway such that they were lent money at call on an unsecured basis. The separation of liability (loan) from corresponding asset (collateral) meant that there was room for slack in ensuring that the credit was channelled into sound investments.

Meanwhile, an amendment to English company law made it much easier to set up limited liability companies. Prior to 1862 their formation had only been possible by special charter. The prospect of limited liability and unlimited profit soon unleashed a craze among investors – hundreds of companies were formed, the majority of which would fail. When excessive issuance made shares a tougher sell, companies issued acceptance notes, a form of 'promise to pay at a future date' – these acceptance notes were then discounted at discount houses to raise the money required. However, these acceptance notes were not like bills of exchange in that they were covered by the sale of goods at a fixed future date. Rather they were backed by a promise of an income stream generated by the company; an income stream which was susceptible to some fantastical extrapolation.

As the older partners ceded control to younger, more inexperienced partners, Overend, Gurney and Co. funnelled the money that banks were lending to it in the money market into financing these speculative companies by discounting their acceptances. Then, early in 1866 news emerged of company failures that would spell losses for the discount house. Further rumours started to circulate about the quality of its asset base and its ability to meet its call and deposit liabilities. The rumours soon escalated into a run on the firm. When the discount bank asked the Bank of England for assistance by way of a loan, the Bank declined on grounds that the firm had offered insufficient collateral. It did not help that the economic climate was one in which, after a period of speculative excess, a lot of investments were turning sour. Unable to secure the cash to honour its payments, Overend, Gurney and Co. failed, defaulting on nearly £19 million of liabilities in the process.

The failure caused an acute crisis of confidence among other banks and the ensuing panic was of unprecedented proportions.

It came close to rupturing the entire credit structure of the economy as short-term loans in the money market made to discount houses were part of the reserve money of the banking system. All major financial institutions found their solvency called into question and were vulnerable to a cascade of runs. The demand for liquidity soared and as bankers drew upon their deposits held at the Bank of England's Banking department, it saw its own cash reserve plunge by almost half in the course of a day, not only limiting its ability to act as lender of last resort but also threatening its viability as a bank that could meet the claims of its customers.

The panic was so great that the government had to temporarily suspend the Act of 1844 to give the Bank the authority to exceed the statutory limit on note issuance, allowing it to meet both customer liabilities as well as act as supplier of credit. To guard against any inflationary bias, it required the Bank to raise its bank rate to 10 per cent. News of the suspension calmed the situation and confidence returned as it became clear that there was to be no shortage of cash at the Bank. However, while deposits flowed back into the Bank, the banking institutions continued to be under stress. Further failures were not avoided, and indeed only heightened the withdrawal of deposits from other solvent banks, which in turn failed as they were not able to raise cash quickly enough. It took three months for the crisis conditions to end, but normalcy did not come soon enough to avoid a severe dent to business and savings.

Following the economic cost of the crisis of 1866, Walter Bagehot, then editor of *The Economist*, wrote of the importance of the Bank accepting its role as lender of last resort.[4] Its job as supplier of credit in times of crisis fell upon it naturally by virtue of its unique position as the reserve manager of all other banks.

The mere acknowledgement of its role, he wrote, would act to prevent uncertainty and panic:

> That in time of panic, it [the Bank of England] must advance freely and vigorously to the public out of the reserve. For this purpose there are two rules: First. That these loans should only be made at a very high rate of interest. This will operate as a heavy fine on unreasonable timidity, and will prevent the greatest number of applications by persons who do not require it. The rate should be raised early in the panic, so that the fine may be paid early; that no one may borrow out of idle precaution without paying well for it; that the Banking reserve may be protected as far as possible. Secondly. That at this rate these advances should be made on all good banking securities, and as largely as the public ask for them. The object is to stay alarm, and nothing therefore should be done to cause alarm. But the way to cause alarm is to refuse someone who has good security to offer.
>
> The news of this will spread in an instant through all the money market at a moment of terror; no one can say exactly who carries it, but in half an hour it will be carried on all sides, and will intensify the terror everywhere... If it is known that the Bank of England is freely advancing on what in ordinary times is reckoned a good security – on what is then commonly pledged and easily convertible – the alarm of the solvent merchants and bankers will be stayed. But if securities, really good and usually convertible,

are refused by the Bank, the alarm will not abate, the other loans made will fail in obtaining their end, and the panic will become worse and worse.

The Bank nonetheless shied away from a formal acknowledgement of its role as lender of last resort as it entailed a commitment to keep a larger than usual reserve of 'unused capital' at hand to aid other banks that seemingly over-risked their capital to earn profits. It preferred to rely upon the temporary suspension of the Act of 1844 to allow it to break the fixed issue limit in order to meet a panic demand for liquidity during a crisis. The events of 1890 concerning the near collapse of Barings Bank, however, were proof that, despite the lack of a formal commitment, the Bank of England had understood the counterproductivity of not aiding a financial institution in need of cash against illiquid assets.

Through the late 1880s the Argentine Republic had borrowed vastly from European investors. Barings Bank, a large and prestigious merchant bank, had helped in issuing the debt securities and had itself come to hold a large chunk of it. Then, following a change of government and civil disturbances in 1890, against this backdrop of high indebtedness, Argentina's credit worthiness came into question. As buyers shied away from Argentinian debt securities, Barings was put in a liquidity bind. So it could meet its liabilities, Barings approached the Bank of England for a loan against these illiquid securities. William Lidderdale, the governor of the Bank of England, was aware of the needlessly destructive nature of a panic that a collapse of Barings would unleash. However, Barings' liabilities exceeded £20 million and the Bank of England's reserve was at £11 million, so the risk of potential loss was too large for the Bank to shoulder unaided. Lidderdale approached the chancellor of the exchequer for state aid but his request was declined on the grounds that Parliament would not approve help for a private institution; a temporary suspension of the Act of 1844 in the event of any ensuing panic was deemed more feasible.

Lidderdale's solution was to form a syndicate of financial institutions to jointly guarantee Barings Bank's liabilities to allow it access to funds in the money market. At the same time, he also raised the bank rate to 6 per cent to attract capital and borrowed from the Bank of France and the Imperial Bank of Russia to augment the Bank of England's reserves to better respond to any panic if need be. With the Bank of England's help, Barings survived and was eventually able to cover all its liabilities.

During the Gold Standard era, the general level of prices of goods and services was stable over the long run, but it did fluctuate considerably in the short run. The full Gold Standard was aimed at securing long-run price stability as well as limiting the phenomenon of boom and bust – of inflation and then consequent painful deflation to bring the general price level back down to its long-term constant level – that resulted from excessive issuance in the short-run. The nature of the mechanism put in place by the full Gold Standard was such that shifts in interest rates were dictated by the level of the bank's cash reserve as opposed to the discretion of central bankers.

For instance, say the starting point was one of low interest rates. This inevitably led to increased borrowing and spending, which in due course caused an increase in prices as too much money came to chase too few goods. The Bank of England's cash reserve would then start to fall as people withdrew money from their bank accounts, not only to hold more in their pockets to pay for higher priced goods but also to exchange notes for gold in order to buy foreign currencies, either to pay for cheaper imports or to earn higher rates of return that accrued on them. As the viability of the Bank depended upon the size of its cash reserve, the Bank was forced to hike rates, once it approached a prudent limit.

Similarly, a hike in the bank rate reversed the drain on reserves. It not only attracted foreign savings (in search of higher rates of return) but also contracted business activity such that people demanded fewer goods and services and their prices consequently fell. At higher interest rates and lower domestic prices, people were less inclined to hold cash in their pockets or to buy foreign currencies and left more deposited at the banks to earn a higher rate of return – all factors working to build the Bank's reserve. Once the level of reserve had been restored higher, the mechanism swung in the reverse direction and so on.

The Bank and the government were well aware that the mechanism by which shifts in the bank rate regulated the level of reserves required changes in the real economy: changes that in the event that interest rates needed to be raised resulted in a contraction in the economy and a consequent loss of jobs. But the recurring, relatively small economic cycles were seen as the cost of not just a constant level of general prices in the long run but overall economic stability that resulted from dampened boom and bust.

Over the latter half of the nineteenth century the major world powers increasingly committed to the Gold Standard. This created an international monetary order in which price level movements were transmitted among the countries: a contraction caused by a rate hike in, say, country A was mirrored in country B due to lower imports by A, as well as a retaliatory hike by B to stop an outflow of gold that occurred as capital flew to a higher-rate destination. The emergence of London's merchant banks as providers of international credit granted the Bank of England far more influence on foreign price levels than other central banks.

These British merchant banks acted as financial inter-mediaries between foreign importers and exporters. Though they bought and sold goods directly between themselves, to effect payments, the exporter/seller wrote a bill to the British merchant bank, assigning it the right to 'receive payment' from the importer/buyer. The merchant bank accepted the bill on behalf of the importer for a commission and made the payment to the exporter from its own capital. By accepting these bills of exchange, the merchant bank effectively provided credit to the importer and upon the due date collected the monies from them. A hike in the bank rate by the Bank of England therefore increased the cost of credit for the foreign merchants, which weighed on business activity and demand in the foreign econ-omy, depressing its price level further.

The Bank of England's responsibility at the helm of the international Gold Standard required a deft touch, albeit a differ-ent deftness than that required today. Its task was to adhere to a mechanism rather than to target a variety of economic variables, as today's central bankers are expected to do. In the latter half of the nineteenth century, until the outbreak of the First World

War in 1914, prices were very stable, despite some short-term fluctuations. For instance, the price index[5] for consumer goods and services in Britain stood at 9.8 in both 1875 and 1914, not very far from its level of 10.3 in 1821. Meanwhile, real incomes in Britain quadrupled[6] during the nineteenth century – proof that a constant price level over the long run was conducive to significant economic growth.

The First World War dramatically changed the economic edifice of the previous century. London's merchant banks, as international short-term creditors, were extremely vulnerable to the risk that transacting parties would no longer honour their payment commitments – once a source of influence, they were soon to become a vulnerability. Following the declaration of war between Austria-Hungary and Serbia on 28 July 1914, the merchant banks faced the threat of mass default by their foreign clients unable to fulfil their financial commitments due to the hostilities. The inter-linkages of the credit structure risked the joint-stock banks going under along with them. This fear led to a run on the pound as parties scrambled to withdraw their pounds and convert them to gold in order to ship it out before war conditions made transport untenable. As in previous crises, the Currency and Banking Notes Act was passed on 6 August 1914. This authorised the Bank of England to issue bank notes in excess of its fiduciary limit to meet the panic demand for liquidity. A penal bank rate of discount of 10 per cent was set, as had been customary as a deterrent for inflation.

However, this was a crisis without precedent. A penal bank rate of discount of 10 per cent was seen as excessive and was soon dropped to 5 per cent. Moreover, suspension of the fiduciary limit did not suffice as banks' demand for cash was perceived to be in excess of eligible discountable securities on their books. Also, notes did little to meet the demand for sovereign gold coins by the public, as they only came in larger denominations. The Act therefore also authorised the issue of currency notes of one pound and ten shillings by the Treasury (as opposed to the Bank of England) to serve as legal tender – the banks were allowed to borrow directly from the Treasury as opposed to the Bank of England, up to one-fifth of their deposit liabilities. The bills of exchange that had been accepted by the banks were effectively guaranteed by the government, rendering them a creditworthy instrument that allowed the Bank of England to advance cash against them. The floodgates of monetary finance were opened as the Bank created money to lend directly to the government to fund its war expenditure. As all this superfluous cash found its way into the market, the cost of borrowing fell sharply.

As was to be expected, the surfeit of money at low rates of interest soon resulted in inflation: consumer prices[7] doubled in Britain over the course of the war, and continued to rise after its end. They rose by a further 10 per cent in 1919, and then by another 15 per cent in 1920. The Bank eventually had to raise rates materially to restrain the inflationary spiral. Stability remained elusive, however, as the rate hikes contracted the economy: unemployment spiked to 15 per cent and by 1923 consumer prices had fallen by 26 per cent.

Monetary financing of government expenditure amounted to the effective suspension of the Gold Standard, even though it was not officially suspended in Britain until after the First World War in April 1919. In fact, the onset of the war ended the international monetary order that had maintained the purchasing power of paper money for nearly half a century for the countries that were on it. Though the US stayed on the Gold Standard, the US Federal Reserve began to operate in 1914 in a context that had changed markedly since the time it had been designed. The elastic currency that it had been given to provide liquidity to banks had been intended as a short-run facility to provide financial stability. In the long run, it was assumed by policy makers that the constraints on the stock of money imposed by the Gold Standard mechanism would ensure stable prices. The discipline exacted by the autopilot workings of the international Gold Standard was swiftly replaced by judgement and discretion.

In the immediate aftermath of the outbreak of war, payment for wartime needs triggered an inflationary boom in the US. Upon joining the war in April 1917, the US government both issued public debt and relied on monetary financing to fund its wartime spending. The Federal Reserve acted as its fiscal agent, serving as a bond-selling window and at the same time creating more of its newly ordained elastic currency to lend directly to the government. As in Britain, this proved inflationary, with wholesale prices[8] doubling during the war. Once set in motion, inflation continued unabated even after the war: over the twelve months from May 1919, prices shot up by another 23 per cent.

Nonetheless, the Fed remained initially reluctant to raise interest rates in order to allow the government to issue more cheap debt. It also worried about the impact on the price of government bonds that were held by the commercial banks, which had also loaned large amounts to their customers against the collateral of these securities. It instead hoped that the banks, on their own accord, would see the wisdom of restraint and contract lending. Rates were finally raised in late 1919 and then again sharply early in 1920. These hikes precipitated a severe contraction during 1920–21, and wholesale prices fell by more than 50 per cent within the course of a year. American economists Milton Friedman and Anna Schwartz described the early years of the Fed: 'There was a natural, if regrettable, tendency to wait too long before stepping on the brake, as it were, then to step on the brake too hard, then, when that did not bring monetary expansion to a halt very shortly, to step on the brake yet again.'[9] Though the Fed would soon find a surer footing, discretion still carried the risk of serious errors of judgement.

Under the international Gold Standard, changes in any one central bank's reserve position had dictated synchronised shifts in discount-rate policy of all other central banks, which in turn acted to restrain money supply. However, with the Gold Standard no longer in force and once past the special circumstances of the war years, the question that naturally arose for the Fed was on what basis it was to set its discount policy to determine the quantity of money in supply. The guiding light for the Bank of England had always been the preservation of paper money as a store of value. Constancy of purchasing power as the hallmark of overall economic stability had been centre stage even if the mechanism had put bank reserves in the driving seat in determining where rates were headed. The mechanism in itself was never the goal; in its place any other may have sufficed. It was merely a rule to replace the discretion of central bankers

41

in order to prevent large fluctuations in prices and pronounced boom and bust that resulted from errors in judgement.

The Federal Reserve, however, steered towards an objective that tied in closer to the circumstances of its creation – to prevent disruptions in overall credit availability caused by financial panics. In an echo of the banking principle, it set out to provide continuity of credit to facilitate economic activity. It dismissed the notion of price stability as a focal point, stating in the guide to credit policy in its annual report of 1923 that 'price fluctuations proceeded from a great variety of causes, most of which lay outside the range of influence of the credit system'.[10]

Consequently, the 'review and determination' of the rate of discount it was to charge for its money evolved to accommodate the needs of commerce and business, which the Federal Reserve Board[11] assessed by looking at a variety of economic facts and banking and credit trends. It was argued that as long as the credit created was restricted to productive uses, as was the case in limiting it to the service of agriculture, industry and trade and not to speculative and investment purposes, its proper function was ensured. In order to protect its credit from being used for speculative purposes, it consequently fell upon the Federal Reserve banks to be acquainted with the loan policies and credit extensions of the commercial banks to which they lent and to supervise them accordingly. The Fed was also cognisant that within each productive field the volume of credit had to be 'justified by a commensurate increase in the Nation's aggregate productivity'.[12] From its origins in ensuring financial stability, the still relatively young Federal Reserve graduated to ensuring adequate access to credit for economic growth, seemingly with the awareness and caveats in place to prevent speculative activity.

Meanwhile, in making purchases of government securities to earn interest on their own account, the Federal Reserve banks soon realised that the sale and purchases of securities on the open market withdrew or put money in the hands of the commercial banks. As this affected their need for cash by way of rediscounting, it needed to become part of monetary policy. In 1922, an Open Market Investment Committee consisting of reserve bank officers was formed to co-ordinate these operations as an integral part of the Fed's monetary policy alongside the setting of the discount rate. Over time, these open market sales and purchases would become the main instrument of regulating money supply, for they gave the Fed the ability to proactively change the amount of funds in the hands of the commercial banks, allowing it to better control credit conditions. In the case of rediscounting, the initiative lay with the commercial banks in demanding credit, one that eventually would come to be associated with financial distress.

Between 1923 and 1929, the US embarked on a six-year period of rapid credit growth and economic expansion. In its 1925 annual report, the Federal Reserve took credit for enabling this expansion by modulating monetary policy to avoid the ebb and flow that was normally dictated by the reserve movements under the international Gold Standard: 'In the absence of provisions for an elastic currency or of ample gold reserves the combined demand during 1925 for currency and for gold would have made it necessary for banks to reduce their loans to borrowers.'[13] As events unfolded, however, policy discretion would soon be bedevilled by unintended consequences and bad timing.

On the other side of the Atlantic, the price volatility of the post-war years in Britain created a yearning for the economic stability of the Gold Standard era. Consequently, Britain restored the Gold Standard in 1925, although, as would become evident later, the price of gold was set too high. An overvalued pound meant it was cheaper to buy foreign goods and the demand for British goods fell, causing an outflow of gold. The economy contracted at the same time and unemployment rose.

By the second half of 1927, Britain's economy found itself trapped in a depression with double-digit unemployment. Unable to relax rates to preserve its gold reserves, the Bank of England requested help from the Federal Reserve, asking it to lower its interest rate in order to make it less desirable for gold to flow out of Britain, which would in turn allow the Bank to do the same. The US economy was facing a mild slowdown of its own after an expansionary spurt, so the Fed readily obliged with a lower discount rate and hefty purchases of government securities on the open market, which was to prove excessive, as was admitted by a member of the Federal Reserve Board in 1931:

> In the year 1927... you will note the pronounced increase in these holdings [Federal Reserve holdings of United States securities] in the second half of the year. Coupled with the heavy purchases of acceptances it was the greatest and boldest operation ever undertaken by the Federal Reserve System, and, in my judgement, resulted in one of the most costly errors committed by it or any other banking system in the last 75 years![14]

In the short term, low interest rates fended off an economic slowdown and helped restore Britain's position. Unfortunately, it also unleashed a further expansion of credit and an ill-fated bull market in stocks fuelled by speculative loans – a boom that did not show up in consumer prices and eventually ended in an unprecedented bust.

To its merit, early in 1928 the Fed registered its alarm at the rapid rise in the level of borrowing by banks against securities, and it started to tighten monetary conditions. By mid-year, the discount rate was raised from 3.5 to 5 per cent, alongside sales of government securities on the open market. However, while these measures restrained credit growth for a few months, they ultimately proved inadequate to stall the up climb. In the first half of 1929, as loans to finance the purchase of securities continued to fuel rampant stock market speculation, the reserve banks and the Federal Reserve Board began to argue about how to respond. Bankers at the Federal Reserve Bank of New York wanted decisive action by way of discount rate hikes and open market operations. The Board, however, worried about the effect of higher rates on valid commerce and hoped that better sense would prevail among investors so that they would abstain from betting in the stock market.

As the arguments continued, the stock market surged by 25 per cent between June and August 1929. This fuelled yet further demand for security loans, most of which were now being provided by non-banking lenders (investment trusts and trading companies). In August 1929, the Federal Reserve Bank of New York raised its discount rate again from 5 to 6 per cent. As the economy started to slow from its peak earlier in the summer, the ebullient stock market was ready for an almighty correction.

The popular post-mortem on the Wall Street Crash focused on the irrationality of investors and the lack of decisive interest rate hikes to curb speculation, caused by a clash of personalities between bankers at the New York Federal Reserve and those on the Board of the Fed. There was insufficient acknowledgement of the well-documented role of low interest rates in boosting asset prices and the justifiable speculation that this inevitably sets off. In fact, some eighty-five years on, central bankers still barely acknowledge the causal relation between the interest rate and a disproportional frenzy in the real estate, stock and credit markets rather than the real economy.

Friedman and Schwartz referred to the Federal Reserve's discretion in ensuring financial and economic stability in the mid-1920s as the 'high tide' of its efficacy. But British economist Lionel Robbins, in his book *The Great Depression*, issued a more accurate if damning verdict: 'it was deliberate co-operation between Central bankers, deliberate "reflation" on the part of the Federal Reserve authorities, which produced the worst phase of this stupendous fluctuation'.[15] An attempt to iron out the minor ebb and flow of economic activity created an impressive expansion in the economy, but also set the stage for a contraction of equal amplitude: 'It was not old-fashioned practice but new-fashioned theory which was responsible for the excesses of the American disaster'.[16] But what plagued the conscience of the central bankers in the years to come was not what they did, but what they did not do.

By early 1929, a combination of the increase in US interest rates and an accumulation of gold by the Bank of France had started to take a toll on the Bank of England's reserves. With the further aim of discouraging British investors from speculating on Wall Street and helping to curb the stock market frenzy, the Bank of England raised its bank rate to 5.5 per cent. Then, in September 1929, the collapse of a large British finance company led to a sharp drop in confidence among British investors on Wall Street. Soon after, the Bank of England raised the bank rate from 5.5 to 6.5 per cent to halt the outflow of gold – a measure that aggravated the global slowdown in economic activity already in place. These events finally culminated in the stock market crash on Wall Street in the last week of October 1929 – by mid-November, the stock market had fallen by 40 per cent from its highs.

Between 1929 and 1933 in the US – the period referred to as the Great Depression – nominal GDP[17] fell by 45 per cent, consumer prices fell by 25 per cent and one in four people in the labour force was out of work. In its annual report of 1933, the Federal Reserve claimed that from 1930 to 1933 it 'pursued a policy of liberal open-market purchases, which at first helped the banks to meet extraordinary demands upon them and later to build up excess reserves to an unprecedented level'.[18] However, successive waves of bank failures that started in the autumn of 1930 and continued into 1931, and then occurred again in 1933, rendered a different verdict on the US Federal Reserve.

The suspension of a bank in New York and one in Philadelphia in October 1930 sparked off panic withdrawals from other banks in Kentucky, Tennessee, Arkansas and North Carolina, triggering several more failures. As banks continued to fail, deposit holders became ever more anxious and the panic withdrawal of cash only gathered momentum. Bank assets had declined due to the contraction in economic activity that had followed the fall in confidence after the stock market crash.

However, the distressed sale of bank assets – loans and investments – precipitated by the panic cash withdrawals contributed to the price declines and contraction of credit. Prices plummeted and businesses closed and defaulted on their debts, for the want of liquidity that the Fed as lender of last resort was supposed to provide. These declines put further pressure on the banks, leading ultimately to an unprecedented collapse of the financial system. Between December 1929 and February 1933, over one in every five banks failed in the US, a total of 5,500.

In 1931, developments in Europe added to the worsening economic mood. In May of that year, Austria's largest private bank, the Creditanstalt, shuttered down and triggered a run on the German banking system. In turn, British banks had their assets held in these banks frozen. A run on sterling soon followed, and the Bank of England, faced with outflows of gold, raised its bank rate from 2.5 to 4.5 per cent in July 1931. With unemployment at over 20 per cent and a shrinking economy, Britain's commitment to the Gold Standard (which would have required further rate hikes to halt the gold outflow) was cast into doubt and the run on the pound continued unabated. Convertibility to gold was subsequently suspended in September 1931, and though the bank rate was hiked to 6 per cent to ward off fears of inflation, it was soon slashed to 2 per cent in June 1932 where it remained until November 1951, except for a brief interlude at 4 per cent at the start of the Second World War.

Under pressure from Congress, meanwhile, the Fed briefly undertook large-scale purchases of government securities in April 1932 with the aim of increasing commercial bank reserves in order to make them more inclined to lend to boost economic activity. But this only provided temporary relief to the economy, and another wave of bank failures developed by the end of the year, triggering a full-scale panic in early 1933. In the face of panic demand from depositors, banks in several states imposed state-wide bank restrictions intended to halt the withdrawal. In the meantime, these banks acted to shore up their cash reserves by withdrawing from their own accounts in correspondent banks in other states that had not restricted access: as a result, banks in other states, chiefly New York, faced an acute drain on their funds. Rumours of an impending devaluation of the gold value of the dollar further increased the demand for gold and other currencies, intensifying the stress on the New York banks and the Federal Reserve system. In a bid to halt the panic, on 4 March 1933, a state-wide suspension of banking activity was declared by the governors of New York, Illinois, Massachusetts, New Jersey and Pennsylvania. The Federal Reserve banks joined in and remained closed on that day as well: 'the central banking system, set up primarily to render impossible the restriction of payments by commercial banks, itself joined the commercial banks in a more widespread, complete, and economically disturbing restriction of payments than had ever been experienced in the history of the country'.[19]

The paralysis that the Federal Reserve suffered in preventing successive bank failures, and the insensitivity of the Bank of England to the contracting impact of high interest rates, soon cost both these prestigious institutions their operational independence. The events had a lasting impact on the psyche of the modern-day Fed and the Bank of England. The lesson they took away from the turbulent years of the Great Depression was to err forever on the side of keeping interest rates low rather than be found guilty of inaction. Ironically, this thinking would eventually cause these central banks to replicate the collapse, rather than avoid it.

Immediately after taking office on 3 March 1933, the new US president, Franklin D. Roosevelt, declared a nationwide suspension of banking activities from midnight on 6 March to 9 March. This was to allow for a comprehensive review of all the banks following which only sound banks that were in a position to meet customer claims were to open, thereby restoring public confidence. On 9 March, Congress passed an Emergency Banking Act to authorise the president to take such necessary measures, which included the temporary suspension of gold payments and the emergency issue of Federal Reserve bank notes to meet the liquidity needs of the banking system. This was the beginning of Roosevelt's 'New Deal' policies, aimed at economic recovery and reform of the banking system. It also marked the end of the Federal Reserve's operational independence.

The role of the Fed was now to enable the government to obtain cheap rates of financing of its spending to help the economy recover. As sales and purchases of government debt securities on the open market were the mainstay of monetary policy, this role followed as a natural consequence. At the outbreak of the Second World War, the Federal Reserve began to buy government debt securities to protect their prices from disorderly declines and keep their yields[20] from spiking higher. Once the US entered the war, the Fed publicly committed to a bond price support programme to facilitate low interest rates on government debt securities to enable the Treasury to obtain cheap finance. It committed to maintain the interest rate on long-term US government bonds between 2 and 2.5 per cent and to buy unlimited amounts of three-month Treasury bills at a yield of 0.375 per cent.

Scarred by the human toll of high unemployment during the Great Depression and faced with the prospect of thousands of returning soldiers, US Congress passed the Employment Act in 1946, tasking the government with promoting maximum employment, production and purchasing power. The Federal Reserve continued its bond support policy to aid with this task, even after the war. The resultant surge in inflation, however, made the complete relegation of monetary policy to the needs of government financing untenable and the Fed finally won back its operational independence after a hiatus of nearly two decades. In March 1951, the US Treasury and the Federal Reserve reached an accord; while they recognised the need for on-going co-operation, they agreed to withdraw support for government bond prices in an attempt to 'minimize the monetization of public debt'.[21]

In the UK, it took even longer for the Bank of England to get its independence back. Such was the public disenchantment with the legacy of high interest rates associated with the resumption of the Gold Standard in 1925 that the Bank of England (which was nationalised in 1946) did not recover its operational independence from the Treasury until over fifty years later. Interest rates were set to facilitate full employment and cheap government finance within the constraints posed by inflation and fixed exchange rates.

The economic ideology of the post-war years saw a dramatic shift. Inflation was no longer seen as an unmitigated curse. Rather it was viewed as the 'cost' of mass employment. Prevailing theory argued that there existed a trade-off between unemployment and inflation; more inflation meant less unemployment. As alleviating the economic suffering of the public was considered more important than preserving the sanctity of the currency, inflation became permissible so long as it was kept in relative check.

The theme of government spending supported by low interest rates, in an effort to ensure full employment, continued through the 1950s and 1960s in the US. The Federal Reserve kept up its promise of co-operation but nonetheless acted to contain the rate of consumer price inflation at no more than low single digits each year. With real GDP growth in the US averaging 4 per cent annually from 1950 to 1970, the theory that greater economic activity and higher levels of employment came at the cost of inflation was nicely validated.

But the understanding that a trade-off existed between inflation and unemployment was undermined by chronic high inflation in the 1970s. Going against received wisdom, higher rates of inflation were now also accompanied by higher unemployment. As the 1970s continued, inflation became increasingly irksome. The primary focus of monetary policy shifted: now its goal was to control inflation with an eye to maintaining growth, rather than the other way round. By 1979, following the appointment of Paul Volcker as its head, the Federal Reserve's annual report stated: 'The primary goals of monetary policy in 1979 were to curb inflationary expectations at home and maintain the value of the dollar abroad without exacerbating recessionary tendencies.'[22] In the war on inflation, the aim of maintaining maximum growth had not only been demoted to second place, but had also been progressively downgraded to an effort just not to worsen any recessionary tendencies. By the mid-1980s, consumer price inflation had fallen dramatically: from an average of almost 10 per cent per annum between 1978 and 1982 to a little less than 4 per cent between 1983 and 1989. Volcker had not only successfully won the inflation battle but also affirmed the merit of the Fed's operational independence.

With inflation under control, the emboldened Fed that emerged under the leadership of Alan Greenspan in 1987 shifted the policy focus again: switching back to an emphasis on economic growth yet very mindful of the importance of price stability as being the most conducive element for growth over the long term. At the same time, the Fed remained eager to prove that it had learned the lessons of the Great Depression and now understood the importance of financial stability. The 30 per cent crash in the Standard & Poor (S&P) 500 stock market index in October 1987 presented Greenspan with just the opportunity to prove this. The Fed provided ample liquidity to the banking system, demonstrating that it was in the business of preventing any lasting consequences of financial instability on economic growth.

Britain's experience with inflation in the same period was even harder: its retail price index[23] rose by an average of 10 per cent per year in the 1970s and 1980s. This paved the way for inflation targeting by an independent central bank. In 1992, Norman Lamont, then chancellor of the exchequer, set the inflation target at 2 per cent, and in May 1997 his successor Gordon Brown announced that the government was giving the Bank of England operational independence to set interest rates. The 1998 Bank of England Act made this effective and set the central bank's task as being to secure price stability and 'subject to that, to support the economic policy of Her Majesty's government, including its objectives for growth and employment'.[24]

The chastising impact of runaway inflation had led to a melding of traditions: the Bank of England returned to its roots in ensuring price stability while being aware of the need to support growth and employment at the same time. The Federal Reserve, meanwhile, focused on ensuring maximum economic growth but within the confines of price stability. An implicit element of growth and price stability was to ensure the provision of credit by the banking system to the economy. This came with the responsibility of close supervision of the banking industry and a thorough understanding of its asset base, allowing it the ability to act with speed and confidence as a supplier of credit in its role as lender of last resort: a role so eloquently described by Bagehot in 1873 and painfully reiterated by the Great Depression.

And so it happened. Born of a *quid pro quo* between a government and shareholders and the exigencies of banking panics, the central banks had shed their mortal skins and by the 1990s emerged as the three-headed Supreme Beings they are today – Controllers of Inflation, Overseers of the Financial Industry and Creators of Economic Fortunes. Shaped by experience of a turbulent century and blessed with the circumstance of tamed inflation, the Fed would earnestly start to play the game of bluff with its three objectives in mind. The Bank of England would follow its lead. History, however, had been waiting to repeat itself, in the hope perhaps that this time around, they would learn not just from what they didn't do but also from what they did.

Part II

The Game of Bluff

4

The *Kung Fu Panda* Effect

In the DreamWorks animated movie *Kung Fu Panda*, Po is a panda who, via a series of adventures and mishaps, inadvertently comes to be anointed as the 'Dragon Warrior' tasked with ensuring peace in the land. With the title comes coveted access to the Dragon Scroll, which contains the secret key to limitless power that he needs to defeat the evil snow leopard Tai Lung. But when he unfurls it, he finds it to be a reflective blank surface.

Let down by the scroll and disheartened by the enormity of his task, Po resigns himself to a life running his father's noodle shop, famous for its 'Secret Ingredient Soup'. To try to get him excited about running the noodle shop, his father, Mr Ping, decides to share his carefully guarded trade secret.

Mr Ping reveals that in fact there is no secret ingredient in his special soup but that it suffices to simply tell people there is, since all it takes for something to be special is for you to believe it to be so. The key to limitless power dawns upon Po and he realises what he must do to defeat Tai Lung.

The central banks' ability to affect economic outcomes is much like Mr Ping's soup – it exists essentially because the public believes in their special ability to do so. As long as the central banks can create an aura of confidence that they have what it takes to defeat economic recessions, the bluff works to validate itself.

Imagine, for instance, that in a year's time you will receive an income of $110 from a benefactor. In the absence of a facility to borrow, you would have to wait for a year in order to receive the money before you could spend it. However, as a market for borrowers and lenders exists, you may bring forward the expenditure of this future income. Assuming a prevailing cost of borrowing in the market of 10 per cent per annum, the 'present value' of that income today is $100 – present value being the opposite of the more easily understood concept of simple interest, which poses it as $100 invested today at 10 per cent amounts to $110 in a year's time. Then, in anticipation of $110 in a year's time, you may borrow its present value of $100 today, which you can then spend over the course of the year and still repay the loan plus interest ($100 + $10 = $110) when you finally receive the money. If the cost of borrowing for a year were to fall from 10 to 5 per cent, the present value of your expected income would jump from $100 to $105, allowing you to spend more of your future income today while still permitting you to fulfil your obligation of repayment of principal and interest to the creditor who allows you this facility.

Suppose now that your benefactor, while otherwise kind, also happens to be a little moody and unpredictable. Your $110 of income in the future is now uncertain, and so your behaviour must change accordingly. If, for instance, you start to believe that your $110 in a year's time may fall to, say, $55, then the present value of that income at 10 per cent interest is no more than $50 today. A fall in the cost of borrowing to 5 per cent bumps up that figure to $52.[1] However, it is the lower amount of future income that dominates how much you are able to spend today. If you come to suspect that your benefactor will pay you nothing, then a lower cost of borrowing is useless to you. While the central bank may be in a position to push down the cost of borrowing, how much of an income you expect to receive in the first place is a factor outside its control unless it can somehow convince or intimidate your benefactor into being more charitable and/or make you believe that it can do so.

Similarly, imagine you can rent a factory for a year for $90. You borrow the money you need at an interest cost of $9 (a 10 per cent cost of borrowing), and then sell the goods you produce in the factory for $100. If the central bank lowers its interest rate such that the cost of borrowing halves, then your profit increases by $4.50, allowing you to invest more in the business. However, if you are uncertain about the demand for your goods and worry that you will only sell $80 worth of output, then the anticipated profit and investment disappear.

The lower the confidence in a future income stream, the weaker is the power of a lower cost of credit to encourage spending and investment. How rich you feel today, or how much you spend in the hope of future earnings, depends not just on the interest rate, but also on what you believe your future income will be. The central bank can drop the interest rate all the way down to almost zero, or even make it negative. But for it to affect your behaviour you must believe that there is the potential for a strong income stream to begin with. As soon as your confidence in that potential income stream starts to wane, the central bank starts to lose its ability to defeat economic recessions.

The psychological hold that the central banks have over us that allows them to influence our assessment of our future income is as important as the actual cost and availability of credit, if not more so. The central banks must impress upon us that when they lower interest rates, better economic times will shortly be upon us. The greater the Pavlovian association we make between lower interest rates and a spurt in collective spending, the less the central banks have then to eventually act.

Their psychological hold on the public may be intangible but it is far from flimsy. The structure of the economy gives them a considerable advantage in exercising their influence on us and pulling off their bluff. Our belief in the central banks' special ability to affect economic outcomes stems from their control of money supply by using the commercial banks as a conduit for lending.

Essentially, the public deals with the commercial banks, which in turn deal with the central banks. A commercial bank[2] is required to hold only a fraction of its customer deposits as a cash reserve to meet customer withdrawals; a fraction set by the central bank and held in an account with them (or as vault cash). Then, any minimum reserve level dictates[3] the amount the commercial bank may lend. For instance, if customers deposit $1,000 in a bank and the reserve requirement is 10 per cent, the commercial bank can lend $900. If the central bank lends against or purchases debt securities from the commercial bank, it must in return pay cash, which then gets credited into its reserve account. Once in possession of more cash reserves, in excess of the required minimum set by the central bank, the commercial bank has more to lend to the borrowing public, who in turn spends what it has just borrowed.

As these spending proceeds get deposited in other banks by those who earn them, it creates yet more lending. For example, if the central bank credits a commercial bank's account with $100, it then can lend out $90, say, to a shoe manufacturer, who then spends it all on raw materials. These monies are then deposited in the accounts of the sellers of the raw materials. So these other banks can then lend out $81 against these new deposits, and so on. An increase in bank reserves above the mandated requirement can thus potentially deliver a stream of money through the economy as people borrow and spend on goods and services.

So when the central bank wants the commercial banks to lend more, it lowers its short-term lending rate to the commercial banks and credits their accounts with more cash in excess of required reserves by buying government debt securities – usually (though not limited to) Treasury bills of very short-term maturity. As purchases raise the price of these securities, their yield consequently comes down; more cash in excess of required reserves therefore comes with a fall in the interest rate on short-term government securities as well.

As commercial banks can borrow more cheaply from the central bank, they are therefore more inclined to charge lower rates to private borrowers. Equally this short-term rate is also what the commercial banks can earn on their balances held in their accounts at the central bank. So when the rate comes down, they have less desire to hold any cash above the required minimum with the central bank and are incentivised to lend any excess reserves to riskier borrowers to earn a higher rate of interest. Therefore, each time the central bank conducts open market purchases and lowers its short-term lending rate, there is a natural push for commercial banks to lend more and at cheaper rates to private borrowers.

Nonetheless, for the commercial banks to lend, they must be willing to undertake the risk of lending for private profit, as there must also be a desire by the borrower to take on more debt. If for whatever reason they remain unwilling and the commercial banks end up holding on to their excess cash reserves, the central banks can ultimately bypass them by printing notes and distributing them directly to the public, much like distributors of free newspapers who stand at street corners handing out copies to passers-by. People then have more in their pockets to spend, without the obligation of debt. Moreover, the incentive for people to hold and spend this money is higher, as their banks now pay them a lower return on deposits.

In essence, one way or another the central banks can find a way to pump money into the economy. If the quantity of money that the public has access to increases, while the quantity of real goods and services remains the same, what follows is that people start chasing up prices with superfluous cash, and we experience a rise in prices.

The central banks' power to affect the money supply is real and its impact is forceful. The greater wherewithal of commercial banks to lend, the manna of a lower cost of borrowing and a rising general price level that aids business profitability are all visible, tangible results. The key, however, to the central banks' seemingly limitless power lies in making us believe that printing money and cheap debt are the means to everlasting prosperity.

5

A Medicinal Dose of Inflation

T he Gold Standard had ensured that, notwithstanding some fluctuation in the short term, prices were stable over the long run, thereby ensuring that paper money acted as a store of value as well as a medium of exchange. The intellectual consensus as well as the political reality that emerged post-Second World War came to accept some perennial loss of purchasing power as the inevitable cost of creating jobs. However, the runaway inflation of the 1970s coalesced opinion once again on the importance of price stability as a necessary precondition for growth over the long run.

But while the Gold Standard had ensured that a pound in Britain had roughly the same purchasing power in 1914 as nearly a century earlier, the omnipotent central banks came to cheat a little. Instead of aiming for a currency that *fully* retains its value over time, it allowed itself a positive target for some measure of consumer price inflation, whether explicit in the case of the Bank of England or implicit[1] in the case of the US Federal Reserve. This was not to be a huge amount from one year to the next, but just a passable 2 per cent per annum. So if $100 bought 100 apples in one year, the following year the same $100 would buy only 98 apples. Moreover, as long as the short-term rate of interest set by the central banks was *at least equal* to that of inflation, the holder of that $100 need only put his money in an interest-bearing account to be made 'whole' in real terms at the end of the year. Nominally, he would be richer by $2 – but in reality his $102 could still buy him just 100 apples.

It goes without saying that if you were to know that money were to lose purchasing power by 2 per cent a year, you would do the necessary to ensure that you earned a rate of return that compensated for it. Hence, if you were to loan money to someone, you would ensure that you were compensated for at least the loss of purchasing power, if not more, for the risk of lending to them. Also, if you were an employee, you would equally want to ensure that your wages adjusted for the rate of inflation each year.

It is of little surprise therefore, as Knut Wicksell, widely accepted as a pioneering monetary economist, pointed out, that 'if a gradual rise in prices, in accordance with an approximately known schedule, could be reckoned on with certainty, it would be taken into account in all current business contracts; with the result that its supposed beneficial influence would necessarily be reduced to a minimum'.[2] Therefore a debtor would not benefit from the loss of purchasing power of money that allows them to produce only 98 apples to pay off $100 of debt in a year's time – the creditor would demand at least $102 in the first place. Similarly, if the 2 per cent inflation rate is factored into wage contracts, there is no advantage to an employer in being able to increase prices for his goods and services while paying his employees fixed wages. So long as everyone was aware that the rate of inflation was 2 per cent, it would make no difference to people as they would act to allow for it. Wicksell compared people who prefer a continually upward moving price level to a stationary one to those who purposely keep their watches a little fast so as to be more certain of catching their trains. 'But to achieve their purpose they must not be conscious or remain conscious of the fact that their watches are fast; otherwise they become accustomed to take the extra few minutes into account and so after all, in spite of their artfulness, arrive too late.'[3]

This leads us to a puzzle. If everyone *knows* that the rate of inflation is going to be 2 per cent, such that they can just adjust the prices they charge, then it is at best innocuous and at worst a pointless distraction. Why then, if targeting a known rate of inflation makes no difference, did the central banks choose to aim for 2 per cent, when they could have set a target of no inflation at all and saved everyone the hassle of allowing for it?

The seeming desirability of a rising price level comes in reaction to the threat of deflation to an economy that has any reasonable level of indebtedness. If consumer prices deflate or fall over time, a country's currency gains purchasing power in the same period. So in a year's time $100 would buy 105 apples if the rate of price change was minus 5 per cent (in other words, prices fell by 5 per cent over the year). The corollary to this is that a given nominal amount of debt would snowball in real terms over time. So one would have to produce more apples in a year (105 instead of 100 in our example) to earn enough to pay off the original $100 debt. As deflation increases the real burden of debt over time, it weighs upon business profitability and leads to job losses, leading to lower income and demand, which in turn pushes prices lower, further increasing the real burden of debt.

It therefore perpetuates economic depressions. While it is clear that deflation is undesirable and that inflation may be desirable (provided that the lender was somehow fooled into not allowing for it in the first place) in the context of a heavy debt burden, it still does not solve the puzzle of why a rising price level, the rate of which can be anticipated, is to be preferred to no inflation.

The real reason is to allow the central bank a tool of discretion. Under normal circumstances, the government has no intention of inflating and debasing its currency. So with a known rate of inflation that people can factor into their economic dealings, it makes no difference as savers and lenders act to requisitely allow for it. However, when the central bank decides that a 'loss of purchasing power' is needed, so long as there exists a rate of inflation that is above zero it has the ability to inflict it. It does so by merely setting its short-term lending rate below that of inflation, effectively creating a negative real rate of return. This makes for a most brilliant, psychological sleight of hand. For the effective loss of purchasing power does not come by a rise in the inflation rate. The rate of inflation at 2 per cent remains the same, a fact of life that the public has been accustomed to, making it irrelevant. The loss of purchasing power comes via a fall in the compensation that is required to render savers whole in real terms. It is a mind trick that makes the public more acquiescent to a loss of purchasing power; it is not the rate of inflation that has gone up, rather it is the rate of return that has fallen. This gives the central banks a key advantage over the old stratagem of obvious inflation by governments. As inflation is politically sensitive, it can prove fatal for a sitting government in a democracy. Moreover, it also runs the risk of rebellion on the part of lenders, who may come to expect even further inflation and consequently raise the rates of return they need to lend for longer periods disproportionately higher. If, however, the rate of inflation is always 2 per cent, then inflation expectations are inclined to always stay at the same level. Ostensibly, the promise is of a 2 per cent inflation target, and indeed the central bank, on behalf of the government, does not falter from delivering it. The target is so well anchored in the public's mind that even when the rate of inflation spikes above it, the public dismisses it as temporary for it has no reason to doubt that the central bank will move away from its announced intention. However, from the perspective of creating an effective loss of purchasing power by taking away the compensatory rate of return, the job is nevertheless very systematically and efficiently done.

The question that naturally arises is why the central bank wishes to create this loss of purchasing power. It does so as it deems it necessary to cure a slump in economic activity. As doubt and hesitation that people feel about each other's spending and hiring plans have a self-perpetuating element, a loss of purchasing power is meant as coercion to induce them to overcome it. It makes them take risks when they do not wish to. For instance, if the rate of return that a commercial bank pays on interest-bearing accounts and return on short-term government debt securities is lowered to zero when the rate of inflation is 2 per cent, then the effective or real return becomes minus 2 per cent. The impact of this effectively negative real return on money every year compounds over time. With a 2 per cent rate of inflation, money that bears no interest would *halve in value* every thirty-five years. If a person were to save $100,000 at the age of fifty, their money would have the purchasing power of just $82,000 by the time they were sixty, and just $65,000 by the time they were seventy-two – just at a time when they were thinking of retiring, and enjoying the fruits of all those long years of hard work. So while 2 per cent inflation might sound innocuous, over time it makes quite a big difference, and the need to seek higher returns rises even if it comes at the cost of greater risk.

The saver's loss is the debtor's gain. If an effectively negative return reduces $100,000 of savings to $82,000 in a decade, then equivalently the same applies to the value of debt. This erosion of the real burden of debt that a period of effectively negative interest rates bequeaths the government allows it in turn to borrow and spend more, which only permits it to get the economy out of a slump all the quicker. At the same time, it also effectively relieves future generations from having to pay for past debts.

The redefinition of price stability from a stable price level to a perennial tap of 2 per cent inflation was to give central banks this subtle tool of negative real interest rates. An effective loss of purchasing power was only meant to be a short-term measure, just a timely, medicinal dose to cure the economy of a slump in activity.

6

The Jewel in the Crown

The simple act by a central bank of setting its short-term lending rate below that of inflation sets off a whole series of actions as savers and commercial banks are driven to earn a higher rate of return. Initially the tendency is to continue to lend risk-free to the government, but for extended periods as the rate of return is higher to compensate the lender for locking in their money for longer. For instance, savers may move money out of an instant access current account into a longer-term time deposit for, say, six months or more. In so doing, they are essentially lending to the bank, but as their money is guaranteed by the government up to a certain amount, it remains risk-free up to that limit. Commercial banks and more sophisticated investors with large pools of capital will buy risk-free[1] government debt securities of longer maturity.[2] As rates remain low for longer periods and the effective loss of purchasing power becomes that much more onerous, investors are driven to buy increasingly longer-dated issues. As more investors pile into longer-dated debt securities, their prices increase and as a consequence the extra yield that is offered for locking in money for longer begins to decrease. At this stage, the central bank is well on its way to causing a disproportional rise in the price of risky capital assets that generate future income payments. This ability is indeed the jewel in the crown of the creator of economic fortunes.

Soon, the yield on the longer-dated risk-free bonds does not sufficiently compensate the saver either for the opportunity cost of lending money or the loss of purchasing power, or, for that matter, the risk that neither element of compensation can be known accurately at the point of locking in money for a period of time. This finally drives investors and commercial banks to lend to private borrowers – public corporations and individuals – for increasingly longer periods. As there is a rush of money vying to be lent for higher return, there is a fall in the cost of borrowing for increasingly risky parties.

When banks and investors rush in to lend to risky borrowers, they implicitly make an assumption about the long-run viability of these debtors. Savers (to describe all those with money to invest – commercial banks and different types of investors) in the first instance are driven by the need to protect the purchasing power of their savings. But by no means do they wish to fall from the frying pan into the fire, which they would if the debtor were to go bankrupt and default on them. It is much better to lose effectively just 2 per cent a year than a bigger chunk, if not all of it. Hence, for savers to be keen on lending to risky private borrowers, they must implicitly believe that these debtors will remain viable or money-good and over time earn enough income to have the wherewithal to pay back both principal and interest to them. It's a leap of faith that they must take. And the discomfort of the loss of purchasing power, so cannily engineered by the central bank, makes them more inclined to make this leap of faith and be more lax in their lending criteria. In other words, they fall for the central bank's bluff that when it lowers its short-term lending rate, there will be enough collective economic activity in the future such that otherwise risky borrowers will be able to honour their debt repayment obligations.

Moreover, in lending to risky borrowers for increasingly longer periods, savers lock in returns: returns that may prove to be much lower than those that may come to prevail when central banks raise rates in the future. Hence, in lending to risky borrowers for longer periods, savers make an additional assumption. They assume that central banks will raise rates only when the economy is strong enough to warrant that the risk of lending to these borrowers relative to the government will actually diminish. Hence, there is a minimal opportunity cost of locking in returns by lending to them cheaply.

The decline in long-term lending rates to risky borrowers triggers purchases of capital goods like real estate, improvements in infrastructure and certain types of machines that are built to last and therefore can be seen as generating income *for eternity*. Given their earning potential, these physical capital assets of unlimited durability are naturally expensive, and are therefore normally financed by credit over long periods of time. As the cost of credit goes down, it allows the buyer to pay more for these goods. As in a previous example, for instance, the present value of $110 in a year's time jumps from $100 to $105 when the cost of borrowing falls from 10 to 5 per cent – allowing the recipient of future income to spend more today. Except in the case of these physical capital assets, credit is required not just for one year but for many years. The longer credit is required for, the greater

71

is the price that can be paid for these goods, in lieu of future rental income (or imputed rent in the case of owner-occupied houses), as a consequence of a drop in the cost of credit. Hence, a 1 per cent drop in the cost of borrowing causes a manifold or disproportionate jump in the price of these capital assets.

Consider the following illustration. Say, a property earns $12,000 a year in rent but, at the same time, the owner has to spend $2,000 on maintenance. The net income the owner earns is therefore $10,000 a year. Assuming that the property generates this income forever, the value of the property can be mathematically determined by dividing the annual rental income (after deducting maintenance costs) by the long-term cost of borrowing.[3]

Say, the long-term cost of borrowing is 5 per cent, then we arrive at a valuation of $200,000: $10,000 ÷ 0.05. A more intuitive way of arriving at this result is to calculate the annual rate of return on an investment of $200,000. If the investment then pays a net income of $10,000 in a year, then one has earned a 5 per cent return on initial investment: $10,000 ÷ $200,000. Equally, if an investment of $200,000 pays an annual income of $10,000, then it will take twenty years to pay off the investment. This is just the inverse of stating that the rate of return is 5 per cent per year, as 1 ÷ 20 = 0.05, or 5 per cent.

If the cost of borrowing for the same property falls to 4 per cent, then the value of property is 10,000 ÷ 0.04, or $250,000. Provided that the net rental income remains at $10,000 per year, a drop in the cost of borrowing from 5 per cent to 4 per cent results in a spectacular increase of 25 per cent in the value of the property. Those who attribute the increase in house prices we have seen in the past two decades to irrational crowd behaviour should think again. It is the result of a lower cost of borrowing carefully engineered by the central bank.

Similarly, a fall in the prevailing cost of borrowing faced by corporations causes a disproportional rise in the price of corporate bonds that were issued by them prior to the drop, in similar fashion to the case of assets that pay an income stream in perpetuity. However, as the series of fixed interest payments made by these corporate bonds are limited to only a number of years in the future, the increase in price, though still disproportional, is less pronounced.

It is fair to conclude that a fall in the longer-term cost of borrowing boosts the present value of an infinite stream of dividends as well. Therefore a disproportional rise in the value of the equity market follows suit. However, do the longer-term borrowing costs either for the government or for risky borrowers apply to a share of ownership of a company or the collective equity market?

Let's say you buy into a fund that is invested in all of the large publicly traded companies in an economy and it pays a stream of annual dividends of $1 per share forever. To see the impact of lower interest rates, you must ask yourself how much should you pay for this one share today? If this constant dividend stream of $1 per year forever was as certain as, say, the interest and principal payments on a long-term government bond that yields 5 per cent, one can arrive at the price of one share by calculating the present value by dividing $1 by 0.05 to arrive at a price of $20.[4]

However, this dividend stream is by no means certain as it is a promise or expectation rather than a fixed contractual payment. As that which is uncertain must be worth less today, the rate of interest that you use to arrive at its present value has to be higher. Or in other words, the rate at which you discount future income to attribute it a value today must be higher. How much higher, you may ask? Well, that is a question that only you as an investor can answer. The answer is: as high as you are comfortable with. The cost of borrowing on the market should give you an indication of the implicit trust that lenders have in lending to these companies as a whole. However, it does not suffice fully, as, in the case of bankruptcy, bond holders are paid ahead of equity share owners. Hence, you must require an even higher rate of return than these companies can borrow at on the market. Consider the following illustration. After sussing things out, you decide that, given the risks involved, you need to receive at least 4 per cent more than the yield on long-term government bonds. At this amount of premium for the risk taken (or simply, risk premium), you will feel that you are getting a good enough deal. Hence, in your eyes the required rate of return is 5 per cent plus 4 per cent, or 9 per cent. The correct price of one share is therefore $1 \div 0.09$, or $11.

It is easy to see what happens if the yield[5] on the long-term government bond goes down by, say, 1 per cent. As this is the return you can potentially earn by lending to the government and be absolutely certain of it, it proportionally lowers what you are ready to earn on a risky share. However, let's say that your assessment of how uncertain the dividend payment is does not change and you still require the extra 4 per cent to compensate you for the risk that it may not be paid at all. Consequently, in your eyes the value of one share jumps from $11 to $12.50,[6] about 14 per cent higher – certainly, dispro-portionate relative to a 1 per cent fall in yield, but nothing that makes your eyes pop out, especially in relation to the impact on real estate prices.

The game that central banks are in, however, is to make you believe that that $1 of dividend payment is more certain as a result of their low rate policy and the economic activity that is being generated. And as you believe in their ability, you fall for the bluff and lower the extra risk premium of 4 per cent, down to, say, 2 per cent. That same $1 of dividend payment is now worth over 50 per cent more to you at $17 and therefore you rush to invest.[7] As more and more investors fall for the same reasoning, equity markets unsurprisingly surge yet further. It should be evident that the more investors believe in the potency of rate cuts and decrease the extra compensatory return they require to take risks, the less the central banks need to engineer a drop in the yield on longer-dated government bonds.

Moreover, in reality the dividend of $1 per share is not capped. Companies pay out a ratio of their earnings as dividends. As the economy grows over time, so will their earnings and consequently so will the dividends. What the central bank also hopes to achieve is to make you believe that not only is the dividend more certain but it will also grow at a much higher rate in the future. Again, the effect is the same. The more you believe in the potency of the loss of purchasing power that drives savers into lending and borrowers into borrowing, in order to spend and invest, the more you believe in the ability of the economy and your dividends to grow. As other investors are led to believe the same, the stock market surges even further.

It is usual for investors to extrapolate the current rate at which the economy is growing to make an assessment of what future company earnings and dividends will be. The central bank is likely to be most effective in boosting the equity markets when it has managed to push down the long-term yield on government bonds (say, the yield on a ten-year bond as investors by habit usually pay attention to it) much below the actual or nominal growth rate of the economy.[8] This is when the investor is likely to use this nominal growth rate of the economy as an indication of future earnings, while discounting them at a rate that uses a ten-year risk-free yield that inadequately compensates for real growth and inflation in the economy. A decent rule of thumb to anticipate strong gains in the equity market therefore is to see how much lower the yield on the ten-year government bond is relative to the rate at which the economy is growing. For this is when investors are led into bumping up the numerator of dividend and lowering the denominator of required rate of return.

Is the central bank wrong in pushing down interest rates and using a loss of purchasing power to propel investors into risky assets? Is it wrong in blustering to make you believe that it will succeed in creating greater economic activity? It says not, as it is only temporary medicine for when you are gripped with fear and unnecessary doubts about the economy's potential. And as a consequence you have raised your risk premium and diminished your expectations of future growth. Is the market wrong in falling for the bluff and believing that future earnings will not only be higher but also more certain? Not necessarily, as negative real interest rates may lead to a higher rate of economic growth, and the actual turn of events may well prove that the investor was correct in assuming the strength of future earnings.

In making you fall for the bluff, the central bank is essentially using the biblical directive *as you believe, so it is done unto you*.[9] We believe in the strength of the economy, and as we become more certain of it, we attribute a higher value to correlated investments where the pay-outs are risky and uncertain. As a result of this belief, our investment portfolios that contain risky assets such as corporate bonds and shares increase in value. The impact of this higher wealth makes us more likely to spend. For instance, if the shares that you hold in your portfolio go up by 30 per cent and bond holdings go up by 10 per cent, the psychological impact of feeling richer is tremendous even if you are unlikely to immediately realise your gains. Moreover, it reduces the imperative for you to save more of your current income, making more available for you to spend today. You are consequently more susceptible to splurging on some new shoes, buying a few books in the local bookshop or going out for a nice dinner with some friends. Consequently, the shoe seller, the bookseller and the restaurant owner are all richer as a result of your spending. As they now have more income, they in turn spend more. And so on.

Higher house prices set off an even more powerful impetus to spend. They allow those with more equity in their property to borrow against these elevated values. The extra spending that this borrowing permits – whether for home improvements, holidays or whatever – similarly allows for more growth in the economy. Higher asset values boost the wealth not just of householders but of companies and banks as well. Companies can borrow more on the back of stronger balance sheets, and not only are banks eager to lend them more as a result, but the increased asset values on their own balance sheets makes it easier for them to do so.

Normally the values of shares and real estate react to growth, but in this case growth is a *consequence* of the increase in these asset prices, engineered by lower interest rates. The bluff is smoothly done. As with the question of the chicken and the egg, it is never really apparent which came first: the rise in asset prices or the economic growth that supposedly propelled it. The starting point of this self-fulfilling dynamic, however, was belief, and as we believed so it was done unto us. If we didn't believe that the economy would grow stronger such that earnings were higher and more certain, we would neutralise the impact of lower rates on long-term, risk-free bonds by demanding a higher risk premium. However, as we believed in future earnings, the value of our investments went higher. And because they went higher, it allowed us to get wealthier and borrow against them and spend, which in turn actually created the growth that we had assumed.

Why is it, then, that equity and real estate prices do not always rise exuberantly in response to lower risk-free interest rates? The short answer is that investors retain the memory of a recent bad experience. Even when long-term risk-free rates are below the rate of growth of the economy, equity investors may simply not fall for the central banks' bluff. In the case of property, lenders may not believe in the capability of the homeowners to come good on their payments, and therefore may not extend credit at all, or at low enough rates to compensate for any fall in rents. It's all a question of belief: for investors, the sting of recent experience makes the central banks less credible. When this occurs, it scuppers the ability of cheap money to impact asset prices.

One way to illustrate investors' 'once bitten, twice shy' attitude is to look at what happened to the S&P 500 US stock market index in 2004 and 2005. In those years, the average yield on the ten-year US Treasury note was approximately two percentage points lower than the nominal growth rate of the US economy. Yet the price appreciation of the S&P 500 index was 9 per cent in 2004 and 3 per cent a year later. Given that the US economy grew at about 6.5 per cent per year, the returns on equity markets were far from excessive. A not unreasonable view is that investors were still smarting from the equity market bust of the early noughties.

But if it's all just a question of what investors believe, what's to say that they are not guilty of unjustifiable exuberance even without the coercive inadequacy of risk-free returns relative to real growth and inflation? This certainly can happen – investors can make erroneously rosy assessments of risky investments relative to reality and imprudently suppress their risk premium even when risk-free rates are adequate. This is indeed the hallmark of a true speculative bubble. This behaviour, however, is rarer than we are led to believe. Significantly higher returns in asset markets relative to economic growth, usually mistaken as speculative bubbles, are more often than not a reaction to long-term risk-free rates jigged expressly lower by the central banks. The central banks continue to manipulate risk-free rates until, frustrated by the inadequacy of return on savings, investors give in to the bluff of a higher future income stream and make riskier investments. There is even academic terminology for this dynamic – it is referred to as the asset price transmission mechanism of monetary policy.

7

The Watchdog

The economy is a motor that runs at a speed and direction determined by its component parts of labour, capital and technology. The motor is, however, oiled by credit that is required to bridge the gap between production and sale and is revved by human emotion. As we expect a society's labour, capital and technology to increase over time, the trajectory of growth is proportionally upward. But because of the vicissitudes of credit and human psychology, growth oscillates along this upward trajectory in a wave-like pattern. Any disruption to the availability of credit, and hit to public confidence, dislodges the economy from its gradually upward path. Equally, a bout of excessive availability of credit and over-optimism sends it hurtling up, away from its sustainable, gradual ascent. As losses from excessive lending are revealed and optimism ebbs, the ups are inevitably followed by downs of mostly – but not necessarily – equal amplitude. The aim of the asset price transmission mechanism of monetary policy is to dampen the amplitude of these waves in a carefully calibrated exercise, with in-built checks and balances. When the economy enters a downspin, the central bank cleverly sets us off on a self-fulfilling journey of believing and actualising: as soon as the public has actualised a more prosperous reality on its own, the central bank takes away the proverbial punchbowl of cheap money. Such is the intention of the art of central banking.

Volatility in financial markets, which is code for a sharp fall (as opposed to both up and down swings) in the prices of financial assets, poses a particular problem. The gash in wealth has the twin impact of suppressing public confidence and lowering the value of credit collateral and consequently risks altering the otherwise upward trajectory of the economy. Cheap money therefore comes in as a handy fix to the problem as it acts to boost asset prices. But how is the central bank to know if its cheap money is not boosting the economy unsustainably beyond its motor's capacity?

The increased spending that results from the new lending and borrowing that follows cheaper money is initially met with increased production of goods and services. So long as demand for goods and services is met with the requisite supply produced by previously unused capacity, prices remain the same. However, there comes a point when all the pool of workers have been employed and the economy is producing all that it can; in other words it is operating at its maximum potential.

However, as businesses still anticipate that demand for their goods and services will continue to increase, they continue to expand and end up having to pay increasingly higher wages to attract workers. This rapid rise in wages then allows these workers to forcefully increase their demand for goods and services. However, as the economy is already at its maximum potential and cannot produce any more, the public ends up chasing a finite quantity of goods and services. The result is that the pace at which consumer prices are rising (or the rate of inflation) accelerates, rising above the targeted 2 per cent level. In a sense, consumer price inflation acts as a sort of economic watchdog – alerting the central bank that the economic engine is as hot as its motor of capital, labour and technology can handle. The central bank's response is to start raising its interest rate, in an attempt to temper expectations of a continued increase in aggregate demand.

To see how this works, consider a situation similar to the US economic experience of the early 2000s. Suppose the economy is doing fine until news hits that, say, serious fraud has been revealed in a publicly traded company with a current market value of $150 billion. Investors' confidence in all companies is consequently badly shaken by the discovery, leading to a 30 per cent crash in the equity market. The loss in wealth leads people to cut back on their spending. Businesses likewise retrench in response – their weaker balance sheets feed into this dynamic, making it difficult for them to borrow and produce. As unemployment rises, household rents (net of maintenance costs) fall by, say, 10 per cent, to $9,000 per annum in the case of the property in our previous example.

Almost simultaneously, the central bank responds by cutting short-term interest rates dramatically. This pulls down the yield on longer-term government bonds. Let's say it falls by 1 per cent down to a level of 3 per cent. Long-term mortgage rates come down by the same amount from, say, an initial 6 to 5 per cent. Despite a 10 per cent fall in net rental income, house prices actually rise by 8 per cent.[1] The economy is still depressed, but banks and entrepreneurs notice this pocket where prices have risen by 8 per cent.

As house prices rise, households that own real estate can sell up and spend the money they make. Alternatively, they can borrow against their properties and use the credit for further spending and investment. Profit-seeking entrepreneurs respond by borrowing money to invest in the real estate sector (which has rising collateral value), and in the process increase their demand for raw materials and labour. The income earned by these newly employed workers is spent on other goods and services: the result is that *businesses across the economy* experience a rise in demand, and start to hire more workers.

Until the pressure of consumer price inflation (measured by an index of choice by the central bank) starts to show signs of acceleration, there is no reason for rates to rise. As long as this inflation is contained at around the 2 per cent target, the virtuous cycle can go on and employment can continue to rise. In the meantime, lenders are more than happy to lend against the collateral of houses. Indeed, given a choice between investing in government bonds that yield 3 per cent and lending at a higher rate, amidst rising house prices, it's no surprise that they opt for the latter. To continue our example, let's say commercial banks drop their mortgage lending rates further to 4 per cent. At the same time, rents rise in proportion to wage growth of, say, 5 per cent. As a result, house prices rise another spectacular 31 per cent.[2]

The consequences of this can be felt across the economy. Corporate profits increase as a result of both lower borrowing costs and higher demand. Equity prices start to rise again. People's net worth increases because of higher house prices and the equity and debt holdings in their investment portfolios, and this propels confidence and spending further. The virtuous cycle sweeps through the economy via the real estate sector – or, more generally, via investment in capital assets that require credit over long periods.

As companies hire more people, the economy starts to reach its full potential, and wages and rents rise over time by, say, a further 20 per cent; cumulatively, nominal wages and house prices have risen by 26 per cent and 51 per cent,[3] respectively. The central bank now starts to raise rates again, such that long-term government yields rise back up to 4 per cent. But mortgage rates only rise to 4.5 per cent, because in better times less of a premium is needed to compensate for the risk of lending. As unemployment falls and the economy reaches maximum potential, consumer price inflation starts to edge up towards 2 per cent and slightly beyond. Satisfied with these results and diligently picking up the signal being relayed by the economic watchdog, the central bank continues its process of normalising the economy by raising interest rates.

8

Financial Markets: Policy Playground or Casino?

The oft-peddled image of financial markets is one of a casino funded by the taxpayer, manned by bankers and played by testosterone-charged traders and investors out for a fast buck. But who, then, is running the casino? While casting aspersions on central banks may not be unjustified, the reason why this popular perception is misleading is because of its projection of financial markets as gambling dens. While traders and investors may appear to be pandering to their gambling instincts, the truth is that their prime motivation to play along with a game orchestrated by the central banks is to protect themselves from financial loss.

Financial markets are no more than a bazaar for assets that are essentially bought with pools of money accumulated by the hard-working public to prepare for an uncertain tomorrow. Savers, which include individuals as well as institutions with large pools of capital such as commercial banks and insurance companies, have a natural tendency to augment their money – either because they only need it in the future and so wish to earn a return to at least preserve its purchasing power or because they want to earn a return higher than their own cost of capital – by lending it to those who need it now, for a price. They therefore come to the marketplace to lend (equally, to buy debt securities issued by those who borrow) their money to those who wish to use it for business enterprise or purchases they cannot afford with their current income. Or they choose to take part ownership in existing enterprise (by buying shares), to share in the income that it generates.

On the other side of the stall are the people who borrow money – the spenders. They pay a price for financial capital, with the aim of eking out a profit over and above what they pay for it, or just to bridge the gap between earnings and expenditure. The biggest borrower is of course the government, which borrows over and above what it collects in taxes from the public so it can fund its expenditure. Then there are companies and individuals, who are borrowing to make ends meet from one month to the next, or to make larger purchases by spreading the cost over a long period.

The two principal groups of entities who come to the market, then, are the savers and the borrowers. The investment banks, which are different from their deposit-taking commercial banking cousins, for the most part act as facilitators, providing services to savers and borrowers to meet their objectives. Their business model is one of charging fees for this facilitation of bringing together savers who are buyers of assets and the borrowers who are issuers of assets.

The power of choice, however, remains with savers. It is their money, and they decide what happens to it: whether they will invest it at all and in what, for how long and, most importantly, at what price. However, although savers appear to be exercising free will over their investment choices, they are in fact being incentivised and sometimes strong-armed by the central banks.

When the central banks set the bank rate or the rate of interest on federal funds – their short-term lending rate to commercial banks – they create a ripple effect on the price of money across the economy. The central banks are focused on buying and selling short-term debt securities issued by their respective governments in order to put their lending rate into effect. However, longer-term interest rates are effectively an average of a string of shorter-term interest rates that will exist in the future. So each time the first few rates change, the longer-term rates experience a pull simply because the earlier numbers in the average have changed. Therefore, when the central bank signals a change in the base rate and holds a press conference to explain its future intentions, the entire government bond market fluctuates, affecting the price and yield of securities with maturity up to thirty years. Moreover, in its press conferences the central bank explicitly tries to influence the expectations that traders and investors have about what short-term interest rates are likely to be in the immediate future and beyond. In so doing, it potentially reinforces the change in price and yield of longer-dated bonds. The continuous movement of prices in financial markets happens because on the one hand the central banks are altering their lending rate, which in effect changes the price of securities held by savers. And on the other, savers are making a very valid attempt of anticipating these changes to avoid being caught offside of the price moves.

Normally, a reasonably sized change in the base rate is enough to drive savers in search of a higher return to bring down longer-term government bond yields and subsequently borrowing costs for riskier borrowers and for risky asset prices to move in the desired fashion. However, each time there is a market crash or a deep recession, savers get more intransigent. They refuse to accept the low levels of compensation for undertaking risk – risk that the central bank deems beneficial for the economy to move towards its maximum potential.

Then central banks have to try a whole lot harder to affect market psychology. When short-term rates are close to zero, the central banks buy a large amount of longer-term government bonds to try to lower long-term risk-free yields. The aim is to frustrate savers with low risk-free yields across all maturities, so they become more inclined to make riskier investments in search of higher returns, while simultaneously increasing the level of reserves held by banks, encouraging them to lend more. When these large-scale purchases involve riskier assets (such as mortgages and asset-backed securities), the central banks skip the private saver as a medium for reducing rates on riskier lending. Instead, they focus on increasing bank reserves by buying these assets and in the process driving up their prices to thereby reduce their yields.

Similarly, the central banks also offer explicit forward guidance about the level at which they will set the base rate for a fixed number of years. Market participants can guess what the central banks will do, but they nevertheless build in some extra yield to allow for the uncertainty that the economy may improve and rates move higher. Explicit forward guidance from the central banks that they will hold rates low until a certain date removes that uncertainty and brings down rates further, as it does away with the need for a yield premium required to compensate for it. Such guidance frustrates savers with low yields on government bonds yet further; at the same time it encourages borrowers to make investment decisions on the assumption that they will enjoy on-going low rates.

Central banks don't want to lower the spectrum of government yields for their own sake; they want them down to boost the creation of credit (that is, lending and borrowing). This requires both savers and borrowers to dance around one another, which in turn requires an optimistic frame of mind. Signalling that rates are to be on hold for a long time risks a counterproductive effect as the public starts to believe that there is something seriously wrong with the economy, which will not permit the central bank to normalise the situation any time soon.

Rather than lowering risk-free rates further, the central bank therefore resorts to further psychological theatrics. It can impress upon the public that its promise to keep rates on hold is valid up until the point that the economy turns around decisively – essentially boasting that its bluff is a sure win. Then, instead of buying longer-term government securities with more of the elastic currency the central bank is entitled to create, it can buy it with cash obtained by selling short-term securities it already holds. As large-scale purchases of government bonds ultimately amount to a monetisation of public debt and could therefore be inflationary, the central bank is wary that investors could counterproductively come to demand higher compensation for lending to the government. The aim in 'selling something' to 'buy another' is to give the impression that the central bank can bring down long-term yields without risking inflation.

The ultimate objective of these tactics is to beat down any resistance from savers who are demanding adequate compensation for undertaking risk. If the tactics don't work, the central bank attempts yet more open intimidation: it commits to large-scale purchases until such time that the resulting influx of cash has brought down borrowing costs to risky borrowers and boosted asset prices requisitely to promote economic growth.

How investors, banks and traders react is a function of the incentives created by the level of risk-free rates, as well as what they come to believe about future economic prospects. The noise and fury of financial markets may make it appear as though they are driven by the apparent free will of investors trying to make a fast buck at the expense of others. However, the actions of the central banks in coaxing a more intransigent, agnostic public in recent years have made apparent that investors were only reacting to the then more subtle signals of monetary policy. If they appeared to be betting in a casino, then they were forced into the game by the central banks, well aware of their sensitivity to being forced to lend to governments at yields perceived as inadequate compensation for the risks involved and opportunities forsaken. And if they were guilty of anything, it was of obediently falling for the bluff that cheap debt and inflation lead to higher income streams that will ultimately sustain the asset prices at their higher valuations.

9

The Jackson Hole Consensus

O ver the course of 1996, the US stock market index – the
S&P 500 – rose by 20 per cent[1] even when the yield
on the ten-year US Treasury note increased by almost
1 per cent. It would be hard to argue that the investing public
was egged on to riskier investments by a long-term risk-free
rate that had been intentionally lowered to undercompensate
the investor. It is fair to say that investors had in effect lowered
their risk premium, to invest in equities based on an optimistic
assessment of the economy.

As it came on the heels of a 34 per cent gain in the year
before, the Federal Reserve was naturally concerned at the prospect that an equity market bubble (a move beyond what the
strength of the economy could justify) was in the making – one
that risked collapsing and triggering an economic decline as in
1929. In a speech in December 1996, the Federal Reserve's then
chairman Alan Greenspan asked how central banks could ascertain whether stock market enthusiasm was justified by economic
strength or was the result of 'irrational exuberance' on the part
of investors. While it was unclear whether he had intended to

temper the market, the label 'irrational exuberance' was soon to become common speak to describe any gains in the stock market that were disproportionately large relative to overall growth in the economy. The role of low interest rates would be curiously unacknowledged even though their impact on capital assets was at the heart of how monetary policy worked.

As the bull market in US stocks charged ahead, the question that vexed central bankers and academics was what policies, if any, should be introduced to potentially curb the stock market and, more generally, risky asset prices. Were these markets something that the central banks were responsible for? In 1999, at the annual symposium hosted by the Federal Reserve Bank of Kansas City in Jackson Hole, Wyoming, two academics – Ben Bernanke (who went on to succeed Greenspan as Fed chairman) and Mark Gertler – offered an answer. Their paper, which validated what had been de facto in practice, lent weight to the majority view that would come to be known as the Jackson Hole consensus.

This consensus among central bankers deemed asset markets to be largely outside their remit. As Bernanke and Gertler explained, targeting or steering asset prices – in the sense of raising interest rates when asset prices rise and reducing rates when prices fall – posed several practical constraints. Central banks were no better than the rest of the market at deciphering what their true value should be, as they had no way of ascertaining which part of asset price rises was justified by the strength of the economy and which a result of over-optimistic expectations. Moreover, their worry was that each time the stock or real estate market went up, the knowledge of an increase in interest rates would have a counterproductive impact on investors' way of thinking. This could unnecessarily depress these markets to a level that was potentially much lower than what jobs and income growth in the economy could otherwise justify. Much as the Federal Reserve Board had worried in 1928 that high interest rates to curb the stock market would punish valid business enterprise, they pointed out that attempting to prick a bubble would negatively impact financial markets and the economy.

The argument ran that because the central banks' focus was inflation, they would inevitably act to contain any potential bubbles in these markets. As higher equity and real estate prices made people feel wealthier, they would be likely to spend more, and once the economy was past its maximal capacity, this would eventually result in inflation. As central banks are committed to controlling inflation, they would consequently raise interest rates. The end result would be a situation wherein higher equity and real estate prices led to higher interest rates. So inevitably, central banks would end up suppressing any exaggerated shifts in asset prices.

The conclusion therefore was that central banks should rely on consumer price inflation to alert them to any exaggerated moves in the equity or real estate markets. 'By focusing on the inflationary and deflationary pressures generated by asset price movements, a central bank effectively responds to the toxic side of booms and busts without getting into the business of deciding what is a fundamental move and what is not,'[2] explained Bernanke and Gertler. Crucially, this approach would absolve the central bankers of making a value judgement as to whether equity and real estate markets were in the throes of speculation or led by economic growth. Instead, it would put in place the rule of inflation to act as rudder. However, as central banks tend to disregard current inflation and act according to their assessment of what it will be in the medium term, it would nonetheless leave it to their discretion as to which moves were to be considered inflationary and which to be deflationary, and to what magnitude.

In reality, their discretion would result in a lopsided policy reaction. Both the Fed and the Bank of England were extremely sensitive to falls in asset prices, on the basis that they risked triggering a deflationary spiral into an economic depression. The ghost of the 1929 stock market crash and the slur of the Fed not having done enough in its wake had left them both forever wary of inaction. So they stood by dutifully, responding to the slightest distress call from financial markets with cheap money as an inducement to sustain risky asset prices.

An asset boom, by contrast, was deemed inflationary only when the increase in spending and hiring that it stimulated went beyond the maximum capacity of the economy. Implicit in this view is that an asset price boom always leads to an increase in aggregate demand for consumer goods and services – even when the defining characteristic of a speculative bubble is that it largely bypasses the real economy and comes to feed upon itself.

There was a tendency for the central banks to view their policy as being merely reactionary to adverse market psychology, in the sense that they were only engineering a fall in long-term risk-free yields when fearful investors had increased the extra compensation they required to take risks. As asset prices acted as a conduit for growth, a fall risked a potential repeat of the 1929 debacle. Therefore, if asset prices got off their track, it was the central banks' role to gently guide them back. As far as the central banks were concerned, they were not inflating asset prices; they were reflating back to a level that they had been at before they were sent off course for whatever reason. Moreover, it was about reflating back to previous levels of economic activity rather than a particular asset class – what mattered was to boost overall economic activity to ensure that there was no permanent dent in spending and employment as a result of an asset bust.

The central banks would overlook the fact that investors were unlikely to be lured into an asset soon after a nasty bust, and therefore their reflation effort was likely to be disproportionately funnelled into a different asset that would go on to become the craze of the day. Instead, they would treat the craze as being merely illustrative of investor confidence, which was not only a prerequisite for growth but also a mark of success of their policy of low rates.

They played a subtle, well-orchestrated game that seemed to have all the necessary in-built checks and balances. And for a while it worked, at times, with almost textbook ease. Until, unfortunately, it went horribly awry.

Part III

A Game Gone Awry

10

The Snag in an Easy Tale

The Gold Standard, after a century of maintaining the purchasing power of money in Britain, was, by the 1930s, guilty of leading the economy into the hangman's noose – throttling economic growth for the sake of price stability. A dramatic fall in prices in the US made for much of the cause and effect of the Great Depression: it increased the real burden of debt that weighed upon profitability, forcing business closures. It was unsurprising, then, that in the post-Second World War era the US and the UK swung in the opposite direction – comfortable in the notion that some loss of purchasing power went hand-in-hand with economic growth – only to find eventually that low interest rates combined with unbridled government spending was a recipe for rising inflation and economic stagnation.

The new, chastened era of implicit or explicit inflation targeting that emerged in the late 1980s and early 1990s seemed to offer the best of both worlds. There was a focus on aggregate demand to fulfil government responsibility of providing maximum employment, alongside a low target for the rate of inflation. These twin goals felt complementary: aggregate demand creating inflation and inflation working as a subtle tool, when needed, to create aggregate demand. When the economy was threatened by recession and the public was inclined to reduce its spending, lower short-term real interest rates would give it a nudge in the right direction. At the same time, lower longer-term risk-free rates and a bit of confident bluster gave equity and real estate prices a boost. This set in motion a virtuous cycle in which banks were happy to lend to individuals and companies with stronger balance sheets, who in turn were happy to borrow against them and spend. The policy appeared to work smoothly, even when economic events posed a significant challenge. The US stock market crash of 1987, steep as it was, left little mark after no time at all. The US recession of the early 1990s, meanwhile, was fixed with a good dose of lower interest rates, which were then raised back up in 1994.

When inflation in both the US and the UK fell dramatically by the mid-1990s, coupled with remarkable economic growth, the challenges of the previous two decades felt like a distant memory. A technology revolution had swept through society, changing the working lives of a global workforce beyond recognition. By the late 1990s, the unemployment rate in the UK had dropped from a little over 10 per cent in 1993 to closer to 6 per cent; in the US, it had fallen below 5 per cent. Inflation in both countries, meanwhile, had fallen to well below 2 per cent. If there was a threat to this halcyon situation, either from economic recession or a crash in global financial markets, the central banks were well prepared for it. They were confident that lower short- and long-term rates to prop up asset prices and aggregate demand would suffice to restore economic and financial stability.

Then in the summer of 1998, Russia defaulted on its debt. The S&P 500 US stock market index declined by just over 20 per cent over July and August, and yields on US Treasuries fell sharply. Long-Term Capital Management (LTCM), a $4.5 billion hedge fund, got caught up in the financial market fluctuations and incurred heavy losses. A collapse of LTCM would risk further market volatility, causing more widespread economic and financial distress. In echoes of what Bank of England governor William Lidderdale had done for Barings Bank in 1890, the Fed urged the major creditors to form a syndicate to provide assistance to LTCM. The firm avoided bankruptcy and a forced liquidation of its fund, which would have exacerbated adverse price fluctuations in financial markets. However, while Lidderdale had at the same time raised the bank rate, the Fed cut its short-term interest rate to sweeten the financial markets, despite a rate of unemployment at just 4.5 per cent. When it did raise rates in July 1999, it did so only in small increments. On both occasions, the Bank of England followed suit. From the low in October 1998 to mid-July 1999, the US S&P 500 index surged by a little over 50 per cent, while the FTSE all-share index (comprising FTSE 350 and small cap indices) rose by over 40 per cent. In both cases, the increases were well ahead of the losses earlier in the summer of 1998 in the wake of the Russian debt default, in what was already a very ebullient stock market.

All this time, unemployment continued to decline in both countries, yet inflation remained low. This was when the game started to go awry. In the period that followed, wages would at best grow at mid-single digits while real estate and equity markets took turns in posting no less than double-digit gains, putting asset and consumer prices on different trajectories.

The central banks saw nothing odd in the fact that consumer prices never seemed to match the froth of certain asset prices. Instead they saw it as normal, because consumer prices only reacted when full employment was reached. Because inflation stayed hemmed in at close to 2 per cent, the implication was that they had perfectly synchronised interest rates to aggregate demand: raising them just in time, well ahead of any overheating of demand beyond the economy's potential. The central banks continued to set interest rates to steer the economy by looking at the pressure gauge of consumer price inflation. All the while, various asset prices would take turns in inflating into seemingly speculative bubbles only to collapse and take the real economy down with them.

Behavioural theorists drew attention to herd behaviour among investors while others would blame it on speculative trading by some. However, what wasn't clear was why human behaviour had suddenly mutated to create a bubble in bubbles when previously such events took place once in a generation, if at all. Even though practitioners, academics and central bankers took the impact of low interest rates on asset valuations as a basic premise in the reflation game, there was insufficient acknowledgement that low interest rate policy was inadvertently responsible for the repeated asset booms and busts. Perhaps the central banks thought they were absolved of responsibility because the lowering of the extra return that investors demanded for investing in risky assets was an expression of their free will. That investors had been strongly incentivised and led on to doing so was something that was glossed over.

The reflation prescription of low interest rates only served as a short-term fix, one that precipitated a relapse into juddering financial volatility with an ever greater impact on the real economy. The issue lay in the disconnect between wage growth and asset prices that rendered the financial system more vulnerable to rising borrowing costs. Moreover, the violent crashes were not caused by a handful of contrarian speculators who used a vantage point to exploit herding investors. For the most part there were very few contrarians left who had not been run over by the stampeding herd that was being goaded on by the central banks. The crash occurred when the herd found itself staring at the chasm between wages and asset prices – and buckled at the prospect of jumping it.

11

Intention Versus Incentives

M r Ping's admission to Po in *Kung Fu Panda* about there being no secret ingredient, and that to make something special you merely have to believe it to be so, may appear as simple, albeit memorable kids' entertainment; hidden in the scriptwriter's words, however, lies the essence of both Eastern and Judaeo-Christian wisdom.

The biblical directive *as you believe, so it is done unto you* indicates that the focal point of our thoughts, whether good or bad, manifests itself in our reality, implying that our beliefs consciously or subconsciously guide our actions. Hence, whether you are special or not special all begins with what you believe. The Upanishads elaborate the same point about the relation between thought, action and outcome with a more positive slant:

> You are what your deep driving desire is,
> As your desire is, so is your will
> As your will is, so is your deed
> And as your deed is, so is your destiny.[1]

As in metaphysics, so in economics. The paradox of thrift argues that if we fret and save excessively for harder times, then harder times will befall us. Each example alludes to the same theme: what we predominantly expect eventually comes to pass simply because we inevitably behave accordingly.

Attempts by the central banks to alter our belief patterns in an effort to create greater prosperity are therefore rooted not just in modern economics but in ancient wisdom as well. Why, then, have these well-intentioned economic warriors left us with a virulent version of boom and bust rather than lasting prosperity? Why have the stock markets and pockets of real estate periodically boomed when higher wages have been so hard to come by? The answer lies in that, by placing the horse of income before the cart of wealth, they create incentives that do not line up with their intentions.

In his 1898 book *Interest and Prices*, Knut Wicksell explained how the disproportionate impact of low interest rates on house prices (or more generally, capital goods which earn their owners an income or a rent in principle, forever) filtered through into higher rents, wages and prices of everything else in the economy:

> It would be possible to raise by anything up to this extent [the extent by which house prices have risen] the prices paid for the materials and services required for house-building. This is based on the assumption that the net earnings of houses (in particular rents) remain unaltered in the future. But there will be a rise in wages, ground rents, etc., and this will bring about a rise in the money demand for all kinds of goods, including houses.[2]

And if it came to pass that low interest rates instead only fuelled an abnormally large amount of investment in such capital goods, then this relative overproduction of houses etc. relative to other goods and services in the economy would only imply 'a more rapid equalisation of relative prices'.[3] This would follow from there being a surfeit of houses for sale, which would weigh upon their prices, while at the same time a relative shortage would lead to a rise in prices of other goods and services. The result, inevitably, would be a rise in prices across the board, not limited just to those of capital goods such as houses.

He described how this increase in prices would feed upon itself and create expectations of further inflation, which would have the same impact as a further easing of credit:

> The upward movement of prices will in some measure 'create its own draught'. When prices have been rising steadily for some time, entrepreneurs will begin to reckon on the basis not merely of the prices already attained, but of a further rise in prices. The effect on supply and demand is clearly the same as that of a corresponding easing of credit.[4]

Wicksell's theories highlighting the disproportionate impact of interest rates on capital goods prices and how it fed into overall inflation were seminal, even if today it is a principle that is taken for granted in the reflationary prescription of lower interest rates. In fact, central banks rely not just on the impact of interest rates on capital goods but more generally on capital assets that include both physical (such as real estate) and financial assets. Moreover, the understanding today goes one step ahead as it assumes that the stimulation of capital asset prices results in more growth, and unwelcome price inflation results only when the economy has reached the point of maximum capacity. By contrast, Wicksell's theories assumed that the economy was already operating at maximum capacity and therefore stressed only the price aspects of the impact of low interest rates.

Nonetheless, it is useful to revisit Wicksell's arguments, if only to highlight a certain granularity that is easily overlooked in the assumed transmission of asset prices by the central banks today. To follow Wicksell's original argument, there should be *an equalisation of relative prices* between those of capital assets and those of consumer goods and services. In fact, implicit in the use of consumer price inflation as a pressure gauge is this equalisation of relative demand and consequently of prices of capital assets and consumer goods and services. The rush that began, say, in housing should lead to a rise in income that should create a proportional increase in demand for all goods and services in the economy. Moreover, as more construction activity takes place, house prices should rise at a relatively slower pace, while the earnings of those who find work in the construction (and other related sectors) boom should cause demand for other goods and services to rise at a faster pace. It is only if this equalisation in demand were to take place that, as the economy approached full employment, the upward movement of prices would eventually be felt in prices of consumer goods and services.

But what if the frenzy in capital assets generated by a lower cost of borrowing was not accompanied by a proportional rise in demand for other goods and services? Imagine for a moment that capital assets are meat, consumer goods are green vegetables and consumer services are complex carbohydrates. Suppose that people are not eating as much as they should to stay healthy. The central bank wants people to eat more – more of everything in healthy proportion. With this intention, let's say that the central bank reduces the price of meat disproportionally: now the public can still eat as much meat as before, but will also have spare cash with which to buy more food. Initially there may be a tendency to splurge on meat as it is relatively cheaper, but then people revert to old habits, thereby proportionately increasing their consumption of carbs and green vegetables as well. However, this is by no means certain. The public may instead increase its meat consumption by a large amount – opting for the fattiest cuts – and leave out the green vegetables and carbs altogether. In the short term, the public may be more sated and may even appear leaner. Longer term, however, such behaviour could lead to a host of serious health issues. In altering the price of meat, the central bank cannot be assured of the desired outcome of a healthier public by virtue of eating more.

Now consider another example. Take three individuals: Mr A has a stable job, earns an average wage, owns his home outright and has reasonable savings; Mr B has an exciting, if risky job, earns considerably higher wages, has a decent stash of savings, and is a bit averse to debt, so prefers to rent for now; finally, Ms C, who has lost her job in the recent recession, and has meagre savings. Suppose that the central bank cuts short-term interest rates to close to zero, prices are rising at 2 per cent every year, and the long-term cost of borrowing has fallen. How are each of these individuals likely to behave?

Ms C will be forced to live off her savings, spending it on consumables and rent out of necessity – somewhat independently of the nudge of rising prices – and will hope to find a job in the nick of time. Mr A and Mr B, who are considerably better off, will have more choice. They may nonetheless not be nudged by negative real interest rates into spending more, given that they are happy with their level of consumption to begin with. For instance, say they go running several times a week, and have to get new shoes every twelve months. Do they buy three pairs of running shoes today because they fear that prices will be higher in twelve months? Probably not. If prices go up by 2 per cent, as long as their wages increase by the same amount, they will be able to afford the same price in real terms. If prices go up at a higher rate than their wages, they will likely postpone the decision, gauging whether they can squeeze another few months of wear from their current pair, depending upon their level of confidence in their own prospects at that time. As their basic needs are covered at their current levels of consumption, the incentive to splurge on consumables is low.

Mr A and Mr B will, however, factor in several things. Even if the central bank's aim of 2 per cent holds, prices will still double in thirty-five years. Mr A and Mr B will have picked up on the fact that the central bank – rightly or wrongly – dismissed previous spikes in inflation as transitory and that their earnings may not necessarily keep up. A decade of inflation at an average rate of 3 per cent will diminish the purchasing power of $100,000 to just $74,000 and prices will double in a little less than twenty-four years if that remains the effective pace. This will no doubt lead to a nagging concern that money is not really a store of value and that the economy's debt burden gives the central bank a good motive to be a bit lax with inflation for a few years. And as a result they will act to protect themselves.

Even if they are not financially savvy enough to work this out explicitly, they will have nevertheless noticed that prices are rising even when the rate of return on their savings account has dropped to zero and that their wages are not quite keeping pace. To protect against inflation, rather than splurging on consumer goods and services, Mr A and Mr B will therefore buy assets that they believe will hold up in value against cumulative, long-term inflation.

At the same time, the cost of borrowing is low. Mr A and Mr B are encouraged to take advantage of these low rates. They might, say, invest in a nice house by using their savings as equity to borrow a larger amount, as that would put them in an especially advantageous position should the economy experience short bursts of unanticipated inflation (in case the central bank intends to cheat a little bit more). Mr A may even borrow against his home to finance a second property. Even if Mr B is reluctant to take on debt, he has an incentive to invest his current savings in an asset that he regards as liquid, and which will hold its value in the face of inflation.

Equities as an investment look attractive because inflation increases business earnings, even when it does not lead to rising wages. As investments in gold, art and luxury goods with a strong second-hand market have historically offered protection against inflation, they present attractive alternatives. Those who can, will act to protect themselves from a cumulative loss of purchasing power. Ms C and people like her, however, are unlikely to have the wherewithal to protect themselves, even if they can see the dynamics clearly. Moreover, should opportunity present itself she will certainly buy these capital assets that are visibly appreciating well in excess of anything else.

As their investments appreciate in value, it may be reasonable to expect individuals like Mr A and Mr B to spend some of their capital gains on extra luxuries and holidays. But the incentives are stacked in favour of them investing, and remaining invested, in some form of capital asset. Because the prices of capital assets are rising at rates well ahead of consumer price inflation, that seems a better choice than spending more today, when levels of consumption are relatively healthy. So, for the most part, an increase in credit and money supply will go towards investments in capital assets. Evidence of a drop in savings might suggest a leaning towards increased spending. However, this spending may well be dedicated to higher debt service payments that are linked to larger borrowings to invest in capital assets. Even with unemployment rates at 10 per cent, the remaining 90 per cent who have jobs have an incentive to seek ways to invest to compensate for a loss of purchasing power of any savings as well as for lagging wages. All of this means that – despite the economic theory – the anticipated equalisation in relative demand for capital assets and consumer goods and services does not really take place. Or certainly nowhere near enough to result in an equalisation of the rates at which the prices of both groups grow.

There is no provision either in economic theory or in practice to ensure that the textbook equalisation of relative demand and prices takes place. In fact, contrary to textbook expectation, it is only rational to want to hold on to and chase that which so visibly jumps in price in response to lower interest rates, well in excess of wages and consumer price inflation. The result is a two-tier economy: one that is directly or indirectly engaged in capital assets, and one that engages in the production of all other goods and services.

In light of this skewed pattern, consider what happens to the vast number of companies that are not directly engaged in or linked to the production of capital assets. As they don't see demand for their goods and services rise as much, they are not as keen on expanding and hiring, or at least to a degree that is anywhere as forceful. If these companies are publicly traded they will be encouraged to take advantage of low rates by borrowing money to buy back their stock in the equity market, thereby changing their equity structure to boost earnings per share. Any benefit from lower debt service costs is, however, unlikely to be used to pay higher wages to their staff, even if they hire some more workers to meet the small increase in demand for their product.

The total wage bill for firms engaged in capital assets will be much higher, however, both because the number of workers and the wages per worker have likely increased. Yet this is not enough to define the overall growth of the economy. Overall growth is a weighted average of growth in the capital asset sector and consumer goods and services; the latter sector of consumer goods and services being much larger. As a result, the overall economy and wages earned by workers in aggregate grow at a rate that considerably lags behind that of the asset economy.

To boost the overall economy, if a large swathe of it is lagging, the central bank is then obliged to depend on its conduit of asset prices even more. So it sets out to bolster capital asset prices even further. Yet in the entire basket of available capital assets, there is likely to be one that is blighted by the memory of a recent bust. So the impact of low interest rates is funnelled into one particular asset class, or a subset of the entire basket. This only heightens the imbalance caused by the reflation prescription.

Therefore, even as more workers find jobs, and wages earned by all workers increase to some extent, the upward movement of prices that creates its own up-draught is felt primarily in capital asset prices. *When prices have been rising steadily for some time, market participants act not just on the basis of the prices already attained, but also of a further rise in prices. The effect on supply and demand is the same as that of a corresponding easing of credit, and the asset price boom feeds on itself, even when the central bank has stopped further easing.*

The result of this is that asset prices experience the inflation that was meant to be targeted at people's wages and the price of consumer goods and services they buy. So asset prices, rather than acting as a conduit for growth in the underlying economy, instead represent a monetary phenomenon in themselves as opposed to being value-creating or being the result of value creation. Low interest rates, impending inflation and reasonable levels of current consumption stop people from realising these apparent wealth gains and spending their money proportionately on consumer goods and services. The central bank bluff – to pump up asset prices to support credit creation and encourage people to spend more in the economy – therefore creates a precarious situation in which asset prices are bereft from the economic reality. In this situation asset prices can be sustained at their lofty levels only by low interest rates or by investors who are willing to hold these risky investments without adequate compensation.

12

The Inflation Paradox

In the reviews section on the website of a National Health
Service clinic in central London, an annoyed patient had
left a complaint. Speaking to a nurse on duty, she had asked
to be examined more than once a year for a condition that the
NHS recommends is tested for every three years. The nurse, in
an apparent effort to shake her off, replied that if she was going
to think about the condition so often that she wanted to be
repeatedly tested for it, it was likely that she would then get it as a
consequence of her obsessive preoccupation with it. The woman
had smarted at the suggestion, written up the incident online,
and rated the clinic poorly. The clinic subsequently apologised
and reprimanded the nurse for making the comment.

The nurse may have been insensitive, but perhaps she had
meant it as some well intentioned folksy advice – along the lines
of the biblical maxim *as you believe, so it is done unto you.* The
question whether we are indeed doomed to create what we fear
merely by obsessing over it may be open to debate. But for the
central banks it is a notion that is a lot closer to home. In using
interest rates and their medicinal dose of inflation to ward off

the deathly prospect of deflation and the subsequent increase in the real burden of debt, they actually increase the chances of such a situation occurring.

Consider again our example of the house that generates $10,000 of net rental income a year. A long-term cost of borrowing of 5 per cent implies a market value for the house of $200,000. If the cost of borrowing now drops to 2.5 per cent, a rental stream of $10,000 a year into the future bumps up the value of the property to $400,000. Let's say the happy owner, who has a modest mortgage of $60,000, takes out a loan of another $300,000 against the increased valuation of his house. He spends $100,000 on holidays and other things and prudently uses the remainder as a down payment on a second property. This property also earns $10,000 in net rental income and is worth $400,000; therefore, he needs an additional loan of $200,000. His loan-to-value on his principal property is 90 per cent ($360,000 against a total value of $400,000), but on his second property – which he intends to let out – it is only 50 per cent. His total debt increases from $60,000 to $560,000 against a total property valuation of $800,000.

Suppose that, four years later, the central bank raises its rates and the cost of borrowing goes back up to 5 per cent. The once happy homeowner finds himself in the wretched position of having $560,000 of debt and two houses with values reduced to $200,000 each. The reasoning behind the central bank's move is its assumption that the extra spending generated by lower rates leads to higher wages, which then allows people to pay higher rents. Let's say that during the four years in which rates were low, rents did increase by as much as 20 per cent. That equals a rent of $12,000 on each of our homeowner's properties: at a cost of borrowing of 5 per cent that implies a house value of $240,000.

The homeowner still has negative equity, because together his two houses are worth $480,000, some way below his debt of $560,000. Rents would have to rise by a total of 40 per cent before borrowing costs can go back up to 5 per cent without putting the homeowner into negative equity.

How can rents rise by 40 per cent in four years? Only if people's incomes have risen by the same amount. People earn income in a variety of ways – employment, dividends, interest and rents obtained from the ownership of capital assets, and government handouts. But wages dominate most people's income streams. Rents can therefore rise sustainably only if they are bolstered by a similar rise in wages. If wage growth falls short of the rise in capital assets, then homeowners are at risk of slipping into negative equity when borrowing costs rise (assuming that government handouts stay unchanged).

A house is worth only the rent it generates – which is a function of what people earn – and/or the rate of interest at which homeowners borrow from the bank. Even if the owner does not have any debt against the house, or has locked in the rate of interest that he pays, the current market valuation of the house is determined by the prevailing cost of borrowing and going rents in the marketplace.

Of course, to the extent that our homeowner has not locked in the rate he pays on his mortgage and is exposed to rising rates, his negative equity is made worse by higher interest payments. In response therefore he has less to spend and also tries to save more to try to pay off his debt. If more and more property owners spend less, this in turn reduces the earnings of businesses in general: these companies may then react to their reduced sales by laying off some workers. The banks might then get nervous about lending and raise their borrowing costs independently of the central bank rates. If the cost of borrowing goes up to 5.5 per cent, say, our homeowner's properties fall further in value to $436,000. Our once shrewd property owner now really starts to feel the heat, especially if his boss has just told him there may be a round of cost-cutting at his place of work, and his tenant loses his job and moves to cheaper accommodation. Unable to re-let the house, the property owner instead places it back on the market – a dynamic that is playing out in the rest of the economy. Suddenly, what had looked like a brilliant boom engineered by the central bank, delivering more jobs and 20 per cent wage growth in four years, turns to bust.

The central bank has to start the whole monetary easing process again. This time the commercial banks are not so keen to follow suit – and they have plenty of reasons to be unenthusiastic, given job losses, high debt levels and questionable earning power. As with our homeowner, as people lose their jobs and property prices fall, a surfeit of houses on the market puts further pressure on rents and prices. The downspin of debt deflation is now well in motion – all because the equalisation of capital and consumer relative prices did not really take place adequately, allowing for wages to keep up with asset prices.

So why did the central bank raise interest rates, when it knew that wages had lagged behind capital asset prices and property values were therefore vulnerable? The central bank assumes that even as it raises shorter-term interest rates by many percentage points, longer-term risk-free rates don't rise by as much; this is not unusual as investors perceive long-term rates to be representative of what the economy can withstand in the long run. For instance, if the current base rate is close to zero but the yield on ten-year government debt securities is 3 per cent, then that is where investors think the base rate will be in the future. Therefore, longer-term yields on government bonds may stay relatively unchanged, even as the central bank raises its base rate by several percentage points towards 3 per cent. Moreover, the central bank assumes that low rates of unemployment will encourage the commercial banks and investors to reduce the extra return they demand for lending to private borrowers; hence even with a rising base rate, longer-term borrowing costs in the market do not rise by as much. The central bank also expects that, in light of a stronger economy, company earnings will grow at a higher rate. As a result, stock market investors will be more assured and so along with the lenders will lower their risk premiums. The central bank therefore believes that, in theory, it can raise short-term rates without negatively impacting asset prices. In reality, none of these fortuitous conditions can be taken for granted.

A correction in asset prices caused by a higher cost of borrowing need not always trigger a severe deflationary spiral of lower demand, lower prices and forced asset sales. What determines the severity of the downturn is how much debt householders and businesses have (especially that which has a variable interest rate), which in turn is symptomatic of the extent to which lower interest rates had compensated in the past for the gap between asset prices and wages. The greater the debt burden, the greater the jump in interest payments as borrowing costs rise and so householders and businesses have to cut spending all the more, which spirals through the economy. In addition, the greater the level of debt, the deeper a homeowner falls into negative equity for a given fall in house prices. The psychological burden of negative equity can cause homeowners to cut back on spending even when their monthly interest payments stay the same if they have a fixed rate mortgage.

All this leads us to the unsaid rationale of the Jackson Hole consensus among central bankers. In pre-emptively boosting asset prices so they may serve as conduits for growth, there is inevitably a twilight period in which the former is not justified by the economic reality. The central banks must wait until wages catch up with asset prices and the equalisation of capital and consumer relative prices is fairly advanced. If the central banks were to try to restrain asset prices before the process had led to higher wages, they will have unwittingly doomed the workings of their interest rate medicine.

It is, however, during this waiting period that investors face the strongest incentive to take on more risk than is warranted by the longer-term prospects of the economy. On the one hand they see impressive returns from investing in real estate, equities and risky debt securities, and on the other lies the erosion of purchasing power and little ability to negotiate higher wages. Ironically, the greater this divergence between asset prices and wages grows, the faster wages will then have to rise in order to sustain asset prices in the absence of lower rates.

The central banks therefore are left in a fix: they can knowingly let a bubble grow unsustainably bigger, in the vain hope that wages will catch up in the nick of time. Or they can raise rates in an attempt to restrain the very investor they had egged on, but in the process expose the shaky foundation of the growth they had engineered, thereby risking exactly the deflationary bust they had attempted to prevent. So either way, their low interest rate prescription laced with its inflation aftertaste increases the chances of an eventual deflationary bust. That is the inflation paradox.

13

Speculation Versus Enterprise

John Maynard Keynes was a scathing critic of Wall Street. Writing in the aftermath of the Great Depression precipitated by the 1929 stock market crash, he said: 'The measure of success attained by Wall Street, regarded as an institution of which the proper social purpose is to direct new investment into the most profitable channels in terms of future yield, cannot be claimed as one of the outstanding triumphs of *laissez-faire* capitalism.'[1] The predilection of investment markets, he lamented, was for speculation – investing on the basis of forecasts of market psychology – as opposed to genuine investing based on an analysis of the future income stream generated by enterprise. The US stock market, he wrote, epitomised this tendency and was in fact the national fairground in which people bet according to 'what average opinion believes average opinion to be'.[2]

While it may still be fashionable to speak disparagingly about investment markets, it is naïve to ignore that, in the era of inflation targeting, the onus of directing new investment has shifted from Wall Street (or more generally the community of savers) to the central banks. As central banks can bluff down longer-term borrowing costs to make an otherwise meagre stream of future income from risky investments appear juicy in the short term, the line between what qualifies as speculation and as enterprise is somewhat blurred. The game has long since shifted from betting on 'what average opinion believes average opinion to be' to one of picking up cues from the central banks and responding to the negative real interest rates they set. Average opinion now coalesces to where the central banks want it to go; the threat of an ever greater loss of purchasing power allows them a coercive grip on market psychology.

The ability to borrow allows businesses to bridge the gap between the time of production and when the sale proceeds come in. In the absence of a facility to borrow, only the capital rich would be able to undertake production, and then only to the extent of the money they had. The ability to borrow renders entrepreneurship more egalitarian and at the same time allows more to be invested and as a consequence more to be produced and income to be earned. Similarly, it allows people to bring forward consumption, which creates extra demand. This may well result in more jobs, which in turn creates more demand to support further production. Credit is therefore the 'great enabler' – that vital element that facilitates greater production and consumption and allows for a higher level of economic output and overall income. To prevent a disruption in this essential facility of credit is the underlying premise of the lender of last resort function that lay behind the conception of the US Federal Reserve.

In answer to the question of how much credit is to be created, the Federal Reserve Board provided a guideline in its annual report of 1923: so far as there was a 'commensurate increase in the Nation's aggregate productivity'. In other words, credit is beneficial so long as it allows us to produce more from the same resources. What follows is no more than common sense; if we borrow capital to undertake or augment some productive effort that involves the use of tools, technology and labour, then it must generate income at least equal to the amount we have to repay at the end of the loan period (both principal and interest). Which brings us to credit's alter-ego 'debt' with its negative connotation of being a deadweight burden. What turns credit from being the great enabler into its more insidious alter-ego is the nature of the endeavour it is used to finance. When the investment fails to create adequate value, credit turns into debt that then has to be either written off or inflated away. The more calculated our risk assessment is, the more solid the investment proposition becomes, and the greater is the chance that the money borrowed to finance it is at least paid for and returned over time.

The proactive provisioning of credit through open market purchases by the central banks and negative real interest rates creates a surfeit of cash and enforces risk-taking on the part of the commercial bank and investor. In doing so, it meddles with the assessment of risks as it lulls the bank/investor into taking more risk to earn the same return, in the belief that more collective activity will lead to a greater chance that the borrower will ultimately be able to repay.

For instance, consider that you make the assessment that a house that is worth $100 today will appreciate to $130 in ten years' time because there are more jobs in the economy and greater numbers of families are being formed as a consequence of an increasing population. Hence, you pay $100 today in the hope that it will appreciate to $130. You have only $40 in savings, so to allow you to make the purchase a lender lends you $60 (at 5 per cent per year for a total interest cost of $30) for ten years against the house. This way the lender is assured that if the interest payments fall into arrears and you default on your debt obligation, he is able to recover all of the principal as well as due interest payments by selling the house even at well below its current price. The lender has therefore taken a calculated risk and allowed for a not-so-rosy scenario.

Now let's say that the lender finds himself with a surfeit of cash and borrowing costs on the market have dropped to 3 per cent. He is able to earn only $18 on $60 (over ten years), even when he has, say, $100 in cash. So he lends out $100 for an interest earning of $30 over ten years against the collateral of the same house. But just because the lender is ready to lend more to earn the same interest, this in itself does not necessarily increase the chances that you will be in a position either to service your debt or to repay the money borrowed. It may happen as a result of greater credit creation and economic activity, but not necessarily. In the meantime, the lender is being forced into a riskier undertaking that depends on collective psychology to make it a good one. What may have initially amounted to calculated risk-taking implicit in any business endeavour is rendered largely speculative by the central bank's bluff.

The game of bluff is essentially *ex ante or before the fact speculative* and only, but not necessarily, *ex poste enterprise*. In fact every business endeavour is to some degree speculative, before the effort actually bears fruit. All entrepreneurs must make a leap of faith that they will succeed despite all the provisioning for different risks. And it is only after the event or *ex poste* that one can determine whether it was a good investment or not. However, in inflicting negative real interest rates and creating a surfeit of cash, the central bank changes the leap of faith that goes hand-in-hand with calculated risk-taking into a bet on collective psychology to foster perfect economic outcomes with very little margin for error. Therefore, when risk-taking does not bear fruit and credit turns to debt, it is less because of inept investment decisions on the part of the investor and more because negative real interest rates failed as a remedy.

14

The Fed's Reflation
Prescription in the 1990s

I n the spring of 1990 the movie *Pretty Woman* was released
in cinemas. In the film, Edward Lewis, the character played
by Richard Gere, when he isn't romancing Julia Roberts,
is heavily involved in aggressive corporate activity. In the real
world, such behaviour had indeed left US company balance
sheets in a delicate position. After the corporate profits surge
of 1987–88, mergers, buyouts and share repurchases by companies had effectively swapped equity with debt. The higher
level of debt left companies vulnerable to an adverse economic
environment – a situation that would diminish their revenues while leaving debt service payments the same, or even
higher if creditors raised their rates on a renewed assessment
of lending risk in a worsening economy. With unemployment
falling from about 7 per cent in 1985 to closer to 5 per cent
by 1989, US households had also racked up debt that would
require about 80 per cent of their yearly disposable income[1]
to pay off.

So when recession hit in the summer of 1990, with inflation seen as less of a threat in light of the downturn, the Fed was quick to come to the rescue. It made some hefty cuts in interest rates, reducing them to levels not seen since the 1960s. The Federal Funds rate was cut from 9.75 per cent in 1989 to 3 per cent by September 1992, by which time unemployment had risen back up to a little over 7.5 per cent. The yield on the ten-year US Treasury note fell from a high of 9 per cent in 1990 to a little over 5 per cent by 1993. Consumer price inflation had dropped to close to 3 per cent by then, and continued to slide towards 2 per cent through the mid-1990s.

The interest rate cuts led to economic recovery, with almost textbook elegance. The US economy was growing at an annualised rate of well over 7 per cent[2] when, in February 1994, the Fed started raising rates. The proportion of the population in the labour force was close to its highest since records began in 1948: unemployment, defined as that portion of the labour force (as opposed to portion of population) that was unable to find work, had slid closer to 6 per cent and would continue to fall, reaching 4 per cent by the end of the century. The most significant part of the recovery, however, was that asset prices had not rocketed higher on a separate trajectory. They were being driven by economic growth, rather than remaining contingent on low interest rates. If you had invested $100 in the S&P 500 stock market index and real estate[3] in 1989, by the end of 1994 it would have been worth $130 and $105 respectively, while $100 of US labour earnings[4] would have grown to $128.

By the mid-1990s, unemployment and inflation had both fallen, and Alan Greenspan – having successfully steered the economy out of the 1990–91 recession – had the markets spellbound. As the economy slowed slightly, the Fed started cutting rates again by mid-1995, taking the Federal Funds rate from 6 to 5.25 per cent by early 1996. The fall in the ten-year US Treasury yield, however, delivered far more easing than was obvious from a cut of three-quarters of a percentage point in the short-term rate. It fell by 2 per cent over the course of 1995.

At this point, indebtedness relative to the size of the economy was not growing at an alarming rate. After their late 1980s binge, corporates were relatively sober. US householders, buoyed by good job prospects, were a little more lax but the rise in indebtedness was yet to give cause for concern. However, the hefty fall in long-term risk-free rates triggered a significant move in equity markets: the S&P 500 stock market index rose by 34 per cent over 1995. Then through most of 1996, investors sold US Treasuries to buy equities, effectively lowering their required risk premium.

The continued rise in equity markets by another 20 per cent that year prompted Greenspan's famous speech in December 1996, in which he asked, 'how do we know when irrational exuberance has unduly escalated asset values', as if beckoning markets to question themselves.

'We as central bankers,' he went on to say, 'need not be concerned if a collapsing financial asset bubble does not threaten to impair the real economy, its production, jobs, and price stability. Indeed, the sharp stock market break of 1987 had few negative consequences for the economy. But we should not underestimate or become complacent about the complexity of the interactions of asset markets and the economy. Thus, evaluating shifts in balance sheets generally, and in asset prices particularly, must be an integral part of the development of monetary policy.'[5]

While markets reacted initially to his caution over 'irrational exuberance', they were eventually reassured that the Fed would react to asset prices, and that buttressing them would be an integral part of monetary policy. And so the equity markets marched on.

In the spring of 1997, the central bank raised the Federal Funds rate by a quarter of a per cent to 5.5 per cent, although the subsequent Asian financial crisis put a stop to further rate hikes. Capital that had initially been attracted by higher-yielding investments in Asian countries was being moved back to the US because of the prospect of higher rates of risk-free returns. As real estate and financial markets collapsed in various Asian countries, investors were further attracted to safe assets while fleeing from this volatility, and longer-term US Treasury yields continued to fall throughout 1997. Consumer price inflation fell from 3.3 per cent per year at the end of 1996 to 1.7 per cent by December 1997, offering another reason for a fall in long-term bond yields. The US economy grew by 6 per cent during the year, and the S&P 500 stock market index, buoyed by solid economic growth and lower long-term government yields, appreciated by another 31 per cent. By the end of 1997, $100 invested at the end of 1989 in the S&P 500 index and the housing market had grown to $275 and $114 respectively while labour earnings had risen to $152. The outsized gains in the equity market relative to wage growth were already disconcerting.

By mid-July 1998, the S&P 500 index had risen by another 23 per cent from the start of the year. The decline in inflation that had begun in 1997 had continued throughout the year, and the rate of inflation had slowed to 1.6 per cent per year by the summer of 1998. Consumer price inflation as measured by the

Fed's preferred gauge – the annual change in the price index for personal consumption expenditures – fell below 1 per cent. Unemployment was now down to 4.5 per cent and the proportion of the population as part of the labour force was at a new record high. The disconnect between consumer price inflation and equity prices was not a concern for the Fed; as Greenspan had argued in his 1996 speech, lower sustained inflation meant less uncertainty and therefore higher equity valuations. It was not considered possible that the inflationary impetus had bypassed the real economy altogether, to manifest in the equity market.

In the volatility that ensued in September and October 1998 following the Russian debt default in August, the S&P 500 US stock market index fell by 21 per cent from its July high, taking it marginally lower than where it had been at the start of the year. So when the Fed orchestrated the bailout of LTCM, it threw in several interest rate cuts for good measure as its reflationary prescription. What followed had chilling echoes of 1927 and the period leading up to the stock market crash of October 1929. To borrow from Lionel Robbins' description: a *deliberate reflation on the part of the Federal Reserve authorities* – engineered by a cut in the Federal Funds rate from 5.5 to 4.75 per cent between September and November 1998 – unleashed *the worst phase of this stupendous fluctuation.*

As expected, lower rates had a disproportional impact on equity prices. From its intra-day low in October 1998, the US stock market had surged by 33 per cent by the end of the year, and had appreciated by as much as 27 per cent from its level at the end of 1997. Until the summer of 1998 the NASDAQ composite index comprised of companies in the technology sector had kept pace with the S&P 500 stock market index. In that last quarter, however, it surged by 62 per cent from its intra-day low, posting a 40 per cent gain for the full year.

In the short term, the bluff seemingly succeeded in stimulating growth. The US economy grew at 8.1 per cent[6] – a real return of 6.7 per cent in the last quarter of 1998. Unemployment fell to 4.4 per cent. Corporates bought back their equity shares and issued debt instead to finance the purchase. The reflation prescription had run its magic in just three months. Even so, the Federal Reserve didn't raise rates, because consumer price inflation lay dormant at just 1.5 per cent per year. Once again, there was a chilling parallel with 1927–28, when consumer prices had actually fallen by an average rate of 1.5 per cent per year, alongside a crazed stock market. Before raising rates, the Fed waited for a textbook acceleration in consumer price inflation at the point of full employment.

By May 1999, the S&P 500 stock market index had risen another 11 per cent. Consumer price inflation had finally started to increase, and was rising at an annual rate of 2 per cent when the Fed started raising interest rates in June 1999. It took six months for the Federal Funds rate to get back to 5.5 per cent. During that time, the S&P 500 index went up further and posted a gain of almost 20 per cent for the full year. But the NASDAQ – by now in the grip of a mania that had afflicted investors completely disoriented by the initial impact of the reflation prescription – rose by over 50 per cent over the last six months of 1999, a gain of 86 per cent for the full year. An even more concerning result of the reflation prescription was the continued leveraging by corporates: by the end of 1999, corporate indebtedness relative to the size of the economy had surpassed levels reached in the late 1980s.

By early 2000, unemployment fell further to 4 per cent, and consumer prices finally started to gather momentum, rising at a rate of 2.7 per cent per year. The Fed was satisfied that it had done a great job, not just of reflating the economy but also of taking it to the point of maximum employment that was conducive to price stability. So it decided to apply the brakes. Between January and May 2000 it raised the Federal Funds rate by another 1 per cent to 6.5 per cent. There was a problem, however. Our $100 invested at the end of 1989 in the S&P 500 stock market index and the housing market had now grown to $416 and $130 respectively while $100 of US labour earnings had risen only to $175. The stock market gains had far outstripped wages; the reflation prescription had not delivered the requisite amount of economic growth to support the stock market in the absence of low rates.

The yield on the ten-year US Treasury note had continued to rise throughout 1999, by almost 2 per cent. As it continued to move higher in early 2000, the stock market started to lurch. Investors needed to be convinced that income streams would catch up with the economy – something that many were having trouble believing. However, when ten-year Treasury yields came down in anticipation of another reflationary prescription from the Fed, investors were briefly assuaged: in the summer of 2000, the market surged by 12 per cent from its May low.

Even so, all was not quite as it should be. Higher interest rates exposed the fact that the stock market had been sustained not by adequate growth in the economy but by the magic of a lower discount rate engineered by the Federal Reserve. Given on-going improvements in technology in the 1990s, the NASDAQ became the asset class of the day to be most destabilised by the bluff of a higher earnings stream. By autumn 2000, the descent began in the stock market. Over the next two years, the S&P 500 stock market index fell by 50 per cent and the NASDAQ lost 75 per cent of its value. The pretence of future earnings had evaporated.

15

Reflation Redux

As equity markets fell sharply over the course of 2000, the Federal Reserve worried that a collapse in asset values and deteriorating balance sheets would deter lenders from lending and borrowers from borrowing, and unleash a deflationary contraction. In early 2001, it therefore responded by administering its reflation prescription once again, boldly reducing its Federal Funds rate from 6.5 to 3.5 per cent by late summer. The rate would be slashed again that year in the wake of the Twin Towers attack on September 11: by the end of the year the Federal Funds rate had been cut to 1.75 per cent. Investors were soothed, though not for long: having been burnt in the recent past, they were unwilling to reduce their risk premium for investing in equities. With corporate profits falling for a second year in a row, equity prices started sliding again in early 2002.

Disappointing news in the real economy continued: overall growth in the US was considerably lower in 2001 and 2002, while unemployment rose by 2 per cent. In the summer of 2002 investors' trust took another hit when various large companies were found to be embroiled in fraud and financial impropriety. And just as investors thought the stock market had bottomed out after it fell to half its value just two years earlier, the US-led invasion of Iraq added a whole new level of uncertainty. Equities fell again and the Fed cut rates further to 1.25 per cent in November 2002 and then again to 1 per cent in June 2003. These dramatically lower rates finally buoyed sentiment and in March 2003 equity markets began their ascent once again.

For all the focus on the equity markets, something far more dramatic was happening elsewhere. Until 1997, house price increases had been relatively muted, lagging far behind economic growth and rises in the equity market. US householders already had a fair amount of indebtedness to deal with, and mortgage lending rates had not come down by enough to make more debt affordable. With the albeit modest fall in house prices of the early 1990s still fresh in memory, lagging house prices were, then, of no surprise. As that memory faded, house price rises caught up with economic growth. National house prices,[1] which had risen at about 2 per cent per year in the economic boom years of the mid-1990s, increased by an average of a little over 6 per cent per year over the three years from 1997 to 1999.

When the Fed slashed rates in 2001 to reflate an economy damaged by the stock market collapse, it needed a suitable channel. With corporates retrenching and investors unwilling to fall for the bluff and lower their equity risk premium, the housing market, unblighted by recent negative returns, stood as the ready conduit. As the yield on ten-year US Treasury notes fell from around 7 per cent in January 2000 to a little over 3 per cent in June 2003, long-term mortgage rates (thirty-year fixed mortgage rates) followed suit, dropping from 8 to 5 per cent. The effect on house prices and resulting household debt was dramatic. The fall in borrowing costs had the expected impact – house prices rose 40 per cent over the four years from 2000 to 2003. In the bigger cities, the figures were even more spectacular: house prices in ten main metropolitan cities rose 62 per cent over the same period.

The US house price boom was part of a well-orchestrated reflationary plan by the Fed. It was an important counter to the collapse in the stock market – the value of financial assets[2] held by US households had fallen by $2.4 trillion between 2000 and 2002. The house price inflation fuelled by a drop in borrowing costs engineered by the Fed was thus part of its plan to compensate US households with a rise in wealth that could be monetised into greater spending. As Alan Greenspan described it in his February 2005 testimony to Congress, 'developments in housing markets and home finance' made both the boom and the monetisation of wealth possible. US households were more than compensated for their loss – against the $2.4 trillion dent in financial assets, the value of real estate assets[3] rose by $4.5 trillion between 2000 and 2002. The rise in wealth also ensured that householders didn't need to save as much out of their current income, so were more inclined to boost their expenditure on consumer goods and services.

The real estate asset boom was meant to produce growth, employment and wages – with the rise in unemployment having topped off at a little over 6 per cent, it seemed to have worked. Moreover, as consumer price inflation stayed contained below 2 per cent, there appeared to be no hyperactivity, only capital formation (or more clearly, the formation of capital assets). The Fed had successfully managed yet another episode of financial market volatility without inflicting lasting damage on the real economy. It was more confident than ever in its ability to clean up any further messes should they arise.

In its 1987 annual report, the Federal Reserve had fretted about financial fragility caused by growth in household debt that outstripped disposal income. At that time, household debt had amounted to 80 per cent of annual disposable income. As the gains in house prices were facilitated by borrowing, household debt had risen dramatically. By the end of 2004, it had shot up to almost 120 per cent of income after taxes. Compared with the 1987 annual report, Greenspan's 2005 testimony to Congress focused not on fragility but on the rise in household net worth – the value of the financial and non-financial assets households have, minus their debt liabilities. He pointed out that the rise in indebtedness had come alongside a justifiable increase in wealth. In addition, household liabilities were largely mortgage debt that had bricks and mortar as collateral. Household net worth, Greenspan emphasised, was five and a half times the disposable income.

While this household net worth may have been a source of strength, it was contingent on the value of these assets remaining bulletproof: something that was glossed over and left unacknowledged. The Fed should have picked up on how the level of household indebtedness as a proportion of disposable income was a measure of people's vulnerability to higher interest rates. Instead, Greenspan spoke about the greater affordability of debt resulting from lower borrowing costs and rising incomes. It appeared that the Fed had things under control. Debt service payments made by US householders as a proportion of their disposable income had risen steadily through the late 1990s to

12.5 per cent until the end of 2001. However, as labour earnings grew and borrowing costs decreased, the ratio had edged back down marginally towards 12 per cent by the middle of 2004.

Yet while incomes were growing, they lagged considerably behind growth in house prices. Between 2000 and 2003, labour earnings and household disposable income rose by 19 and 23 per cent respectively, while national house prices rose by 40 per cent. If wages didn't catch up, the only way that this disconnect would not cause house prices to collapse was if long-term government yields stayed low. Or, if they did rise, then lenders fell for the bluff of adequate wage growth in the future, compressing the extra return that they required over and above risk-free rates, and thereby continuing to lend at the same low rates as before.

By the middle of 2004, the US was booming. The economy was growing at an annualised rate of over 6 per cent per year, unemployment had slid back under 6 per cent and the Federal Reserve's consumer price inflation measure was rising at 2.8 per cent a year. The economy had been reflated and the Fed, once again satisfied with the results of its policies, started to raise the Federal Funds rate. It did so slowly, making sure that everyone understood that the pace of increase in future would also be measured. Given that wages needed to catch up with house prices, it needed lenders to be reassured about the future.

In the second half of 2004, the Fed raised the Federal Funds rate from its low of 1 per cent to 2.5 per cent by February 2005. To the Fed's puzzlement, the yield on the ten-year US Treasury note fell at the same time. As the ten-year yield can be seen as an average of consecutive shorter term rates that will exist in the future, it should have experienced an upward pull from the rise in the Federal Funds rate. So the fact that longer-term rates were actually falling in response to a rise in shorter-term interest rates was unusual, because it meant that investors were factoring in a fall in short-term rates further out, contrary to the impression the Fed was relaying in raising its Federal Funds rate.

Expressing his surprise at investors' behaviour in his biannual testimony to Congress in February 2005, Greenspan called the situation a 'conundrum'. One possible explanation was that a greater pool of global savings was fuelling demand for longer-term US Treasury bonds. Greenspan, however, dissatisfied with the various arguments, concluded that bond yields could well be a short-term aberration.

If Greenspan was worried about how low longer-term interest rates were further fuelling the housing market – even though by raising rates he had intended the opposite – then publicly drawing attention to the conundrum had the desired effect. The result was a small sell-off in the bond markets, which caused longer-term yields to rise. This upwards trend, though, was only temporary. From June 2004 to June 2006, the Fed raised the Federal Funds rate by 4.25 per cent: the ten-year Treasury yield[4] and the thirty-year fixed rate mortgage rate rose only by about 1.5 per cent.

The markets knew that the Fed's reflation prescription had created a burden of debt, and that in the absence of wage growth, asset prices were contingent on low interest rates. The ten-year Treasury yield struggled to rise because investors believed that this dead-weight burden of debt and lagging labour earnings meant that there was a limit to how high the Fed could take interest rates – and that if rates did rise beyond this, they would soon have to come down again. As events unfolded, bond market investors were to be proved correct in their assessment. The reason why equity markets rose higher and borrowing costs in the market stayed low was because investors were counting on risk-free rates staying low in the long-run.

Greenspan's 'conundrum' comment was disingenuous. The Fed knew well that in the absence of proportional wage growth, house prices were contingent on low longer-term interest rates. This was confirmed by the slow pace at which it hiked rates, allowing time for wages to catch up and at the same time letting investors believe that it would not do anything to agitate the markets it had inflated to foster the recovery.

In fact, there was no conundrum at all. In any cycle of increasing rates, assuming that there is no uncertainty about the rate of inflation itself, it is reasonable to expect the short-term interest rate and the ten-year rate to converge, to a level that can be sustained over the medium term without derailing the economy. The level to which the Fed increased the interest rate was capped by asset prices, and the short rate and the long rate were converging to that lower terminal rate. The short rate was moving upwards from below this terminal level, while the long rate was moving downwards from above. If the Fed had believed otherwise, it could have increased the pace of the rate increases, taken the short rate much higher and faster, declared its intention, and stood by its assessment that the economy could sustain these rates. The ten-year rate would have converged to the higher level – as it eventually did in 2006, when the Federal Funds rate moved to 5.25 per cent.

In reality, while it was waiting for wages to catch up with asset prices and debt levels, the Federal Reserve needed longer-term Treasury rates to stay down, to persuade lenders and investors to keep the risk premium they required low. Had longer-term rates risen by much more, the subsequent bust would have come sooner, and the Fed would have needed to dish out another dose of its reflation medicine.

The slow pace of the rate hikes in 2004 and 2005 during the period of waiting for wage growth proved fertile ground for the *most stupendous phase* of unsustainable ebullience. During this period, national house prices rose by another 29 per cent – a cumulative 81 per cent since the start of the century when long-term borrowing costs started to fall. House prices in the ten bigger cities rose by a cumulative 38 per cent in 2004 and 2005. Household net worth rose to almost 6.5 times the disposable income, while household indebtedness shot up to 130 per cent of disposable income. At the same time, however, core consumer price inflation[5] measures remained hemmed in at close to 2 per cent. The Fed failed to question why these seriously outsized gains were not filtering through to greater aggregate demand and wage growth.

The Fed had hoped that the real estate boom it had facilitated with its low rates would act as a conduit to sustainable growth. Instead it had developed into an unwieldy bubble. But it was one that could have been contained, even if it was at the cost of a slowdown rather than a greater, more pronounced bust later. In 2004 and 2005, with consumer price inflation rising by over 3 per cent, the Fed had the choice of making sharper rate rises, and at a much faster pace. Essentially, it had two choices. The first was to let the housing market continue unchecked, in the hope that it would decelerate of its own accord, creating higher wages and rents in the process to support the raised prices even at higher interest rates. Alternatively, it could have raised interest rates to a level that would rein in the mania but in the process would have exposed the fragility of high debt burdens and insufficient wage growth it had created. The first choice was more palatable – not only did it suggest a positive outcome, but if it didn't work, the Fed could reflate the economy all over again.

The bust was finally precipitated by higher interest rates and a spike in borrowing costs. It originated with a rise in late payments and defaults among sub-prime borrowers, two-thirds of whom had opted for variable rate mortgages. As rates rose, so did the late payments, causing a spike in the extra return that investors required for the risk of lending. Rises in borrowing costs, together with stagnant rents and wages in a worsening economy, signalled the end of the house price boom. With asset values in free fall, householders were left with a mountain of debt, forcing them to retrench and cut back their spending. This, in turn, slowed down the economy. All bonds backed by mortgages were now suspect. As late payments and defaults rose, banks sustained heavy losses and many even stood to fail. Financial contagion spread as mistrust among lenders grew. The deflationary downspin of distressed asset sales, falling demand and lower prices had begun in earnest. But the Federal Reserve was on hand, with its elastic currency and its reflation prescription of low interest rates.

16

John's House

A commitment to a target by the government, and the operational independence of the Bank of England to ensure it, was to prove so effective a strategy in containing inflation that, by the late 1990s, the prospect of deflation would be as much a problem as price rises. Unfortunately, however, the unruliness of consumer prices of the previous two decades would find expression elsewhere. The more consumer prices were seemingly contained, the more house prices skyrocketed and household indebtedness rose. In the decade after the Bank of England, in 1997, was given independent charge of setting interest rates, housing wealth in England and Wales tripled even while incomes[1] lagged far behind, rising by only half as much.

When the government gave the Bank of England independent control of interest rates in 1997, the Bank inherited a prosperous and stable legacy. The economy had been growing at 5 per cent annually and unemployment had fallen by almost 4 per cent since the height of the recession of the early 1990s. The stock market had risen appreciably in 1995 and

1996, but nonetheless at a more tempered pace than its US counterpart. House prices, meanwhile, had stabilised since their early 1990s fall.

Though consumer goods and services price inflation was running at 1.7 per cent, things were a little more heated in the services sector. The overall figures disguised the fact that the prices of services were rising closer to 4 per cent. As 50 per cent of household expenditure was on services, this couldn't be ignored. Moreover, the slower-rising price of goods reflected the technological advancements that made them cheaper to produce, and the fact that their production was being moved to less expensive locations. The price of services, then, was a better measure of the inflationary impetus in the economy.

The Bank of England, keen to demonstrate its infla-tion-fighting credentials, picked up on this. While the Fed raised its Federal Funds rate by just a quarter of a per cent in early 1997, and left it at 5.5 per cent, the Bank of England raised rates for most of the year, taking its base rate all the way to 7.5 per cent by the summer of 1998. Despite these hikes, the economy grew at a very healthy annualised rate of almost 7 per cent in the first half of 1998.

In the financial turbulence of autumn 1998, as the banks pulled back from lending amidst market volatility, the Bank of England worried about a potential credit crunch. The FTSE all-share equity index fell by almost 15 per cent in August and September, and the Bank was concerned that the drop in equity wealth would hit consumer spending. It was therefore keen to assuage financial markets, even though it thought that the UK economy was less at risk than that of the US. It subsequently decided that 'an early reduction in UK interest rates, following

the easing of policy in the US, would help to reduce current turbulence in financial markets'.[2] Back in 1929 the Bank of England
had followed the Fed, hiking rates even when the British economy was in a depression. This time round, it followed the Fed
in cutting interest rates, even when its own economy was fairly
robust.

While the Fed would cut the Federal Funds rate by
three-quarters of a per cent, the Bank of England cut its bank
rate by 2.5 per cent, lowering it steadily through the summer
of 1999. As in the US, the rate cuts had an immediate and pronounced impact on financial markets and the real economy.
Growth shot up in the last three months of 1998 at an annualised
rate of 9.5 per cent, very similar to the US – by the end of year the
FTSE all-share index had recovered most of its losses of August
and September. Corporate borrowing (in private non-financial
companies) spiked even higher, growing at over twice the rate
of the economy during 1998. If the Bank had worried about
a dampening world economy leading to a credit crunch and
equity market crash, its immediate fears were allayed. Even so,
its concerns remained, and it continued to speed up rate cuts
through the first half of 1999.

In 1999, the stock market rose by 21 per cent. House
prices[3] in England and Wales[4] were up by 12 per cent, and
in greater London by a stellar 22 per cent. Household debt,
meanwhile, grew by 9 per cent, compared with income growth
of just 4 per cent. Meanwhile, corporate borrowing rose by
three times the rate at which the economy was growing. Despite
these figures, the Bank of England took its cue from consumer
price inflation, which dropped to almost 1 per cent over the
course of the year.

Once again, however, inflation in the services sector was at 3.5 per cent, far higher than the 2 per cent target for overall consumer price inflation of both goods and services. Yet whereas that had been a concern in 1997, it was now brushed aside. Equally, while the Bank worried about losses in financial markets affecting lending and spending, it didn't question why these outsized gains in asset values and borrowing weren't being reflected in aggregate demand and inflationary pressure. Or maybe they were showing up in the figure for consumer services inflation, but were being obscured by 'good deflation' in the price of consumer goods. It wasn't until late 1999, a few months after the Fed raised rates, that the Bank raised its bank rate, pushing it up from 5 to 6 per cent by early 2000.

By 2000, the UK stock market – together with its US counterpart – started lurching in response to higher interest rates. The UK, like the US, had shown signs of the exaggerated reflation of asset prices that was unsupported by income growth. Yet the economy held up relatively well: though it slowed towards the end of the year, it still grew at over 6 per cent for the full twelve months; house prices in England and Wales rose by 10 per cent. The stock market was a different story, however. The unravelling of the US equity markets took the FTSE along with it. In response, the Bank of England started cutting rates alongside the Fed in early 2001 – the bank rate had fallen from 6 to 4 per cent by the end of year. The Bank followed the Fed's prescription of reflating asset prices as a fall in their market value threatened spending and credit creation.

British consumers, however, displayed a different character to their American cousins, and proved quite resilient to the stock market declines. Perhaps it was because – as Keynes had remarked of his fellow men – that, compared to Americans, they invested more for income as opposed to capital appreciation. In its August 2001 meeting, the Bank of England acknowledged as much, saying that 'growth in retail sales and in household sector money and borrowing all remained robust, consumer confidence was firm, and the housing market was strong'.[5] Even so, it continued to cut rates, following the Fed as it slashed rates to manage the dark mood in the wake of the 9/11 terror attacks.

By early 2002, even as equity markets were pulled down by the corporate scandals afflicting US companies, John Bull's house was flourishing in all senses. The drop in interest rates in the wake of already robust spending sent things spiralling further upwards. Mortgage rates had fallen by 2 per cent over the preceding two years, encouraging people to borrow more to buy houses. As a result, house prices in England and Wales rose by 24 per cent, while household borrowing rose by 13 per cent that year. Prices of consumer services rose by almost 5 per cent in 2002. But as the combined price inflation for consumer goods and services was running close to 1 per cent, by the middle of 2003 the Bank of England had cut rates further to 3.5 per cent.

In 2003 and 2004, the economy grew at an annual average of a little less than 6 per cent, unemployment slid to a twenty-year low, and labour earnings[6] rose by 5.5 per cent per year. House prices in England and Wales, however, went up cumulatively by another 29 per cent fuelled by a rise in household borrowing.

The pattern that unfolded was very similar to what the Fed had engineered for the US economy. First, the central bank attempted to fix a slowdown with interest rate cuts that used capital assets as conduits for reflation. The capital asset of choice was one that was not blighted by the memory of recent bad experience, so investors were amenable to it. But then the translation of the asset price surge into demand for goods and services was inadequate, leaving wage incomes lagging considerably. Furthermore, because this asset wealth was funded and/or monetised via debt, as in the case of houses, it added to indebtedness. Since the income stream generated by these capital assets depended on the spending power created by wages (which lagged behind), capital asset prices and the greater overall indebtedness had to be sustained by lower interest rates.

In the UK, as prices in the services sector were rising at almost twice the rate the government had mandated, risk-free interest rates on government bonds became increasingly inadequate as compensation. An inflation rate of 4 per cent per year meant that it would take only eighteen years for money to lose half its purchasing power. If the Bank was congratulating itself for anchoring inflation expectations at 2 per cent, it was ignoring the fact that the public was seeking refuge in capital assets to protect itself from much higher levels of it.

Without the equalisation of capital and consumer price inflation, cheap money created disproportionate moves in asset prices, which then needed to be sustained with low interest rates. By the end of 2004, a sum of £100 invested in a house in England and Wales at the end of 1997 was worth £233, while £100 of household disposable income would have grown to just £139. Household debt rose to almost 140 per cent of yearly household disposable income. This lopsided result, created by low interest rates, then had to be equally sustained by them. The mortgage market, meanwhile, was dominated by mortgages that were largely interest only and linked to the bank rate. Or, if they were fixed, then it was only for two to three years, after which they would become variable rate mortgages. This anchoring of mortgage borrowing costs to short-term rather than longer-term interest rates put spending by an indebted consumer in more direct control of the Bank. And if the rate-setting Bank seemed unconcerned by the financial fragility of higher levels of debt, it was partly because it held the indebted nation's heart in its hand.

The Bank started raising its bank rate in November 2003, taking it from a low of 3.5 to 4.75 per cent by August 2004. A year later it would cut it again to 4.5 per cent, where it would stay untouched until July 2006; mortgage rates also remained largely unchanged. In 2005 and 2006, house price rises decelerated to mid-single digits, more in line with the pace at which the economy and incomes were growing. Even so, £100 invested in a house at the end of 1997 was worth £256 by the end of 2006, while £100 of income had grown to just £151 over the same period. A higher starting point meant that even though the rates of growth were in line, the gap between house prices and income levels still widened. This gap was bridged with debt, and by the end of 2006 household indebtedness had risen to close to 150 per cent of yearly disposable income. Meanwhile the corporates, after having repaired their balance sheets – like their US counterparts did in the years following the equity market crash – started borrowing again at almost twice the rate at which the economy was growing.

In August 2006, the Bank started raising its rate again, steadily taking the bank rate from 4.5 to 5.75 per cent by July the following year. In response, mortgage rates started to rise: the two-year fixed rate rose by almost one percentage point, and households with mortgages linked to the base rate now saw their spending money depleted. This, though, wasn't going to be any ordinary rate-hiking cycle: higher rates were soon to expose the fragility of the economy, leading to economic collapse. Over-indebted households and corporates were very susceptible to a spike in borrowing costs, as were asset prices. As indeed was the banking system, and investors who had bought securities that effectively were loans to the households and corporates against the collateral of assets. A fall in the price of those assets, as well as any delinquency on the part of the debtors, left them seriously exposed. As the perceived probability of these scenarios started to increase, it was only natural that the extra return over government bond yields, required by lenders as compensation for greater risk, increased. Mortgage and credit availability became scarcer. The outcome was self-perpetuating. To address the situation the Bank of England cut its bank rate from 5.75 per cent in November 2007 to 5 per cent by April 2008.

Despite all this, 2007 remained a year of reasonable growth. The economy grew at 5.5 per cent, while house prices rose by 6 per cent. The £100 invested in an English house in 1997 was now worth £272, and the equivalent household income figure was £159. Household indebtedness increased steadily, and corporate borrowing continued unabated. By the spring of 2008, however, distressed banks and financial contagion created a credit crunch that precipitated a recession, which deepened significantly by autumn. House prices and equity markets now fell sharply, while borrowing costs and debt defaults travelled in the opposite direction. House prices in England and Wales fell by 14 per cent, bringing the £100 investment in 1997 down to £233 by the end of 2008, while income edged up to £164. The one small upside of the crisis was that for the first time in a decade the gap between house prices and income had narrowed.

Between October 2008 and March 2009, the Bank of England cut its bank rate from 5 per cent to 0.5 per cent. Households and corporates were forced to begin a process of paying off their debt. To compensate for their lack of spending, the government racked up its own debt, though a large part of it was to rescue the ailing banks. By spring, equity markets began to turn around. And as mortgage rates plummeted alongside cuts in the bank rate, house prices stopped falling by mid-2009, ending the year on a modestly positive note. As rate setter, the Bank did have the nation's indebted heart in its hand, after all.

17

Post-Crisis Wrestle

The role of interest rates in the explosion of debt and the spectacular rises in equity and real estate prices in the late 1990s and into the noughties was obscured by what had seemed to be the fanciful extrapolations of delirious crowds. However, the crisis itself – and the post-crisis era – went some way towards exposing the real culprit. The Pavlovian drop in the extra return that investors and lenders demanded for riskier investments each time base rates were cut was something that the central banks had grown accustomed to in controlling asset prices and running the economy with the interest rate lever. Post-crisis, trusting investors and lenders were understandably reluctant to fall for the bluff yet again. This made the central banks' once potent base rate cuts ineffective. As the central banks tried to coax investors into buying risky assets, their increasingly coercive tactics of jigging longer-term risk-free rates and creating inflation at the same time simply revealed that they had been playing this game all along, only with greater subtlety that a more gullible investor had made possible.

The central banks had not fretted about the level of indebt-edness and had instead sought comfort in the fact that house-hold net worth was many multiples of income. This was because they were confident that they could control debt affordability and investors' psychology with the interest rate lever. In the event that lenders raised the risk premium they required, the central banks thought they could lower risk-free rates to compensate. What they had not calculated was that a rise in mortgage delin-quencies by a small minority of borrowers would expose the importance of income streams to asset prices.

This had been the central banks' Achilles heel all along. No matter how much they could boost the present value of a future income stream by lowering the interest rate used to discount it, there could be no discounting of a vanishing income stream. As investors baulked at investing in mortgage-backed securities and other credit instruments, banks that held them on their balance sheets were forced into a liquidity bind. It didn't matter if ultimately these securities proved to be sound investments or not; doubt had spread in the marketplace about their value and this made investors and lenders nervous. British bank Northern Rock found it difficult to obtain the funding it needed, and had to be nationalised in early 2008. Bear Stearns, a US investment bank with large exposure to mortgage-backed securities, was sold to JP Morgan at a substantial discount compared to its pre-crisis trading value.

Alan Greenspan's assessment of 'developments in housing markets and home finance', which had in fact facilitated the translation of cuts in the Federal Funds rate into the real estate boom and surge in consumer spending, had been sanguine for a reason. It was because it had presupposed that this spending would eventually materialise in jobs and adequately proportional incomes. The assumption was that these incomes would then facilitate the servicing of debt and principal repayment. The Fed had not envisioned that a rise in the debt service burden resulting from mortgage rates resetting higher would lead to larger-than-normal defaults because adequate wage growth had not materialised. Nor had it foreseen that the damaging impact of such a scenario was likely to be greater against a backdrop of higher levels of overall debt. Or perhaps if it had imagined the scenario, it had felt confident in the knowledge that as the rate setter it had control of affordability; should indebted home-owners struggle with interest rate payments to an extent that it slowed down the economy, the Fed would be quick to cut rates to alleviate the strain on their budgets. Indeed, it was quick to lower the Federal Funds rate from 5.25 per cent in September 2007 to 2 per cent by April 2008, pretty much reversing all the rate hikes it had made between 2004 and 2006.

But doubt had taken hold of investors, and the Fed's rate cuts failed to ease the grip of fear it had loosened so easily before. The more investors panicked and sold assets, the more the prices of those assets fell. With the collapse of investment bank Lehman Brothers in September 2008, the risk of default rose further, making investors ever more risk-averse. The S&P 500 stock market index lost 50 per cent of its value between May 2008 and March 2009, and the FTSE all-share index was close behind. The risk premium that lenders required for lending to risky borrowers as opposed to the government spiked to three times as much as the year before.

The result was that the Fed cut its rates further, closer to zero, and the Bank of England took its bank rate down to half a per cent. Both also employed various liquidity provision schemes to help financial institutions, effectively swapping illiquid assets for more liquid government Treasury bills or for cash loaned at a penal rate, though only slightly higher than its base rate. The risk that these illiquid assets would ultimately prove worthless now shifted from the financial institutions on to the central banks. However, as they were mere agents, the risk effectively shifted to the respective governments.

Once the base rates were close to zero, both central banks resorted to further monetary easing by way of money creation to buy large quantities of financial assets (mostly government debt securities and mortgage-backed securities issued by US government agencies in the case of the Fed). This allowed them to credit the banks and investors with cash (in lieu of their purchases) that the central banks hoped would be spent on riskier investments. By the end of 2009, this combination – various liquidity provisioning schemes to help the banks, near-zero interest rates and the large-scale purchases of assets – quelled the panic in the market. The most acute phase of the financial crisis was over: equity markets and the price of risky debt instruments had recovered much of their losses. But with mortgages still scarce, house prices continued to fall; the Case-Shiller National Home Price Index lost over a quarter of its value between 2007 and 2011. House prices in Britain also fell, although they fared relatively better.

There then followed a period of repair, in which householders and corporates reduced their debt to become more resilient to the vicissitudes of the economy and the power of lenders. The economy was all the better for it. Central banks had boosted economic growth for a decade beyond what was sustainable, lulling households into spending more by borrowing from future incomes that hadn't grown in proportion. Now it was time to pay down debts by cutting back spending and saving more. Growth would naturally slow down in comparison to what it had been in the heady days of credit-fuelled spending.

But the Fed had expected more. It anticipated a rapid swing back – after all, it had made debt more affordable than ever, and had been willing to support the prices of risky assets by lowering interest rates to zero and then increasing the supply of money through large-scale purchases of securities. So why wasn't the party starting again? Unwilling to accept a slower growth rate, the Fed turned to its old trick of boosting asset prices – even though this had failed to boost incomes the last time around. This, though, was the only way the Fed knew how to act. It was ready to take the chance that the asset price transmission mechanism would work correctly this time around.

Once the acute phase of the 2007–09 financial crisis had ended, the Fed started to wrestle with investors to coerce them back into risky assets – all in the hope that the consequent increase in wealth would get households and corporates borrowing and spending and banks lending with abandon. The central bankers were hooked on speed and fragility, when what was needed was steady, sustainable spending and credit creation that paid for itself.

In the second half of 2010, the Fed announced another round of large-scale purchases of US Treasuries. Householders weren't falling for it: they were not taking on any more debt, if anything they were in pay-down mode. In any case, lenders were a whole lot pickier, so perhaps the slowdown in borrowing was partially forced on to them. The Fed, however, had an easier target: from the time it signalled more monetary easing, the S&P 500 stock market index surged by 30 per cent in just eight months. Then, in the summer of 2011, growth faltered and a crisis involving European sovereign debt unfolded, led by fears of governments' inability to meet their liabilities.

As equities faltered the Fed announced that it would not raise interest rates at least until mid-2013. This was an attempt to bring down the yields on longer-term Treasuries well below inflation to make risky investments look more attractive. The Bank of England announced further asset purchases in October 2011, and another round in February 2012. In December 2011, the European Central Bank came to the aid of the European banking system. Equities recovered their summer losses and gained some further ground. In September 2012, the Fed announced monthly asset purchases for an open-ended time-frame. In August 2013, the Bank of England announced that it would not raise its bank rate from the low of 0.5 per cent, until certain growth criteria were met.

All of these measures were part of a psychological wrestle designed to lower the yields on risk-free government securities. The hope was that inflation would sting investors, pushing them out of the bunker of government bonds into undertaking riskier investments, which in turn would generate jobs, wages and consumer price inflation. The S&P 500 stock market index surged further by almost 30 per cent over 2013. Between October 2011 and the end of 2013, the FTSE all-share index surged by 36 per cent. The central banks were back to bluffing so they could bring down investors' risk premiums. Although it wasn't so easy to convince investors this time around, eventually the central banks won: equity investors responded; house prices turned around in the US and the UK, so much so that 2013 started to look very much like the boom years. All this happened at a time when consumers' incomes in both the US and the UK had grown a lot more than their debt levels: debt as a proportion of disposable income had undone a good bit of the past decade's excesses. Unemployment also fell quite considerably.

For all the good economic news, one old snag remained. Since the turnaround in asset prices, the growth in wages and incomes had again lagged, quite considerably at times. As a result, none of the asset price froth had shown up with any vigour in consumer price inflation; the failed equalisation of the rates of price rises of capital assets and consumer goods and services once again pointing to the counterproductivity of monetary policy. And just as ominously, corporate (non-financial) indebtedness in the US, relative to the size of the economy, had spiked steadily higher since 2012.

By the end of 2014, the central banks were back at the waiting-period juncture, needing wages and incomes to catch up with asset prices so that their values could be sustained at higher interest rates. Nobody likes waiting, though, especially when central banks have conditioned investors to want speed. Investors in particular become impatient when they are not rewarded with large gains. Having been burnt several times, investors are inclined to call the central banks' bluff at the slightest doubt about growth and income prospects and dump their risky assets. Central banks are inclined to turn a blind eye to any excess for fear that they would undo their carefully engineered bluff in the absence of proportional wage growth. However, the more they implicitly encourage, the more investors are prone to using borrowed capital to take risks (to try to make profits in excess of the interest costs), believing that the central banks can fix the problem of lagging wages even if by nothing else than inflation. As investors are conditioned to believe that the central banks will spring into action should asset prices falter for any reason, this only increases the likelihood of excessive risk-taking, which inevitably increases the chances of eventual bust.

Only time will tell which way the latest drama will play out. But there is no doubt that ultimately time will prove that the game of bluff of pumping assets pre-emptively to boost economic growth in the short run is not really worth playing at all.

Part IV

Ramifications

18

A Dark Shadow

A currency that acts as a store of value as well as a medium of exchange, and a smoothly functioning banking system, comprise the basic infrastructure required for an economy to grow. It was only natural, then, that the central banks evolved out of a social contract between citizens and their respective governments to secure this infrastructure.

But then came the Great Depression, the malfunctioning of the Gold Standard, the collapse of the German banking system and the rise of Hitler. Consequently, governments realised that the provision of employment could not be a presumed by-product of basic economic infrastructure. And as jobs were important not just with a view to reducing human suffering but also for the sake of social cohesion, the focus shifted to ensuring full employment. It was only a matter of course that the central banks inherited this duty.

The central banks' policy of catalysing employment relied on interest rates, which acted principally via asset prices. However, as we have seen, this approach failed to generate proportional growth in labour earnings; instead it ended up benefiting those who were already in possession of capital assets. Moreover, in the absence of adequate wage growth, asset prices were at the mercy of investors' appetite for risk and/or low interest rates. They were therefore more susceptible to sudden collapse. However, these assets served as collateral for the creation of credit and as vehicles for savings, so letting them fall once they had been unsustainably pumped up was not an option: it risked eviscerating the financial system and destroying people's savings. The upshot was that interest rates had to stay low to keep these risky asset prices at their higher values.

However, low interest rates had a further redistributive effect of favouring debtors and penalising cash savers. Moreover, a policy that effectively favoured debtors then had an unintended result: it encouraged irresponsible and unproductive credit creation, and raised the probability that this would turn into a pile of bad debt. Restructuring bad debts is not always feasible, especially if they are very large as a proportion of the economy. As the most acceptable way to clear these unproductive debts is for the central banks to engineer a further effective loss of purchasing power, this only reinforced the malfunctioning of the asset price mechanism.

The central bankers glossed over these unintended consequences of their actions. They preferred to focus on the fact that incomes on the whole were larger as a result of using low interest rates to create maximum employment: some amount of bad debts were seen as part and parcel of risk-taking necessary for economic growth, without which incomes would be much lower. As for the redistributive effects, the central banks' argument was that even if the rich were richer, the poor were better off than they would have been without their policy aimed at creating jobs. In fact, any economic policy was likely to benefit some more than others: the case against any particular policy was valid only when one section of society was better off at the cost of another in the sense that the rich get richer while the poor get poorer. So long as this was not the case and the poor were even only slightly better off, then the policy was justified. Rejecting such a policy that allowed for greater incomes (relative to their own starting points) for all, on the grounds that some gained more than others, may result in greater equality. However, that greater equality would only be the result of the rich and poor both being worse off, and the rich losing disproportionally because they had a lot more to lose.

The main purpose in ensuring jobs for all is to give people the ability to pay for food, shelter and other basic material benefits. But given the nature of the human psyche, relative status is very important from the point of view of social cohesion. If hard work and regular employment deliver higher levels of income over time, but lead people to feel increasingly disadvantaged compared with those who own property and means of production, then the effect is corrosive. It will certainly motivate some to go after, and indeed attain, success that is out of the ordinary. However, for the most part, it dooms the vast majority to a sense of drudgery and a feeling that they are 'have nots'.

So, notwithstanding the otherwise logical justification for the unintended consequences of the asset price mechanism, politicians picked up on the aspect of greater inequality that risked social friction – even if their reason for doing so was not to rectify a wrong but because they were afraid of losing out to someone who was ready to use the argument to rouse populist sentiment. They responded by imposing steeper progressive income tax rates on those who earned more, even if they were better paid largely because they had educated themselves to acquire more differentiated skills or had developed talents through greater effort over many years. They penalised those who had inherently chosen the uncertainty of more upside potential (and then had become successful) versus the security of a more humdrum job for life. They would paint all those who contributed more to society with the brush of lazy, undeserving inherited wealth and hence require higher earners to pay not just more (because they earn more) but a greater proportion of what they earn in taxes. Progressive taxation of income earned through hard work, in the misbelief that it is somehow fair, is, however, tacit encouragement to work less hard and in effect be less productive: if workers know that a greater proportion of their marginal earnings is to be paid in taxes to pay for those with more hours of leisure, the disincentive to work longer hours and more productively beyond a certain point is considerably lower. Unfortunately, the disincentive is most effective for the majority who lie at the cusp of when higher marginal rates kick in. Those who make tens of multiples of the average income find ways to avoid it. Moreover, the biggest boost to overall growth would come from incentivising the majority of workers to upgrade their skills and increase their productivity to earn more as opposed to taking from ultra-high earners in the hope that any attempted redistribution will make any difference to the status quo. While higher progressive taxes score very high in populist appeal, they do more damage in effectively reinforcing the fallacy that the majority are condemned to low earnings only because they are outdone by those who use unfair means (and hence must be subject to higher tax rates).

Another rallying call among activists and politicians was for taxes on accumulated wealth. But such a policy would ignore the fact that wealth (to the extent that it was not inherited) was accumulated by saving out of an income that had been subject to higher rates of income tax to begin with, and by investing in assets that have gone up to compensate either for inflation or risk, or because of lower interest rates engineered by the central banks. One could argue for a tax on gains on capital assets that are accrued due to the disproportional impact of lower interest rates, given that these gains do not come from self-effort or risk-taking. But doing so begs the question: instead of taxing asset values back down, why not do away with a deliberate policy channel that pre-emptively pumps them up in the hope of cre-ating economic growth but then fails to foster a stable outcome of proportionate wage growth?

From a practical point of view, given that these asset prices are unstable and subject to sudden collapse, the value of wealth itself is in question, making taxation difficult. Moreover, as any such taxes serve the twin objectives of populist pandering to enhance vote share as well as becoming a lucrative source of income for the government, it gives politicians even less incen-tive to rectify the actual cause of differential growth rates for wealth and income. In Britain such motives are betrayed by the fact that these taxes – either actual or proposed – have often been applied to income and wealth levels that are just above those of the relatively few politicians proposing them.

Given the increasing gap between income and house prices, it becomes imperative to become a property owner at the earliest possible juncture of one's working life. However, the downside is that ownership early in one's career leaves people, at their most productive and daring, saddled with debt, potentially paralysing them into thinking no further than the need to furnish their mortgage payments and hang on to a job that allows them to do so. Property ownership is nonetheless the focal point, as this way people are somewhat protected from the fact that house prices are forever moving further away from their earning capacity; when and if they can afford more, they can sell up and buy a higher-priced property but in the meantime they will have still benefited from the price rise on the one they do own. The pressure and urgency to get on to the property ladder, as it is euphemistically referred to in Britain, is a direct result of the central bank's broken policy of low interest rates. In Britain, as capital gains on the sale of one's main residential property are not taxed while the income tax rate doubles at £32,000[1] from 20 per cent to 40 per cent, there is a clear financial incentive to get on the property ladder rather than to work on promotion or pay rises (the average house price in England and Wales is £192,000[2]). The choice is between saddling the worker with unproductive debt that does nothing for the economy's potential to grow versus incentivising them to earn more, which is the only way to free them from the obsessive compulsion of the property ladder. The government chooses the former in the erroneous belief that its central bank is doing its utmost to facilitate not just home ownership for the people, but also productive credit creation that leads to higher wages.

Moreover, why fix the problem when it offers an easy opportunity for politicians to ostensibly come to the people's aid? What follows are various policies that effectively offer mortgage subsidies that shift the risk from homeowners to taxpayers. It makes lenders more likely to lend larger amounts to homeowners – but it dooms homeowners to the tyranny of debt at a level several times their income. This only creates a precarious liability for taxpayers that would have to be borne by future generations.

One arrives therefore at the absurd situation wherein there are further unintended consequences that result from the redistributive policies to rectify the first set of unintended consequences. Ironically, politicians rationalise redistributive policy measures with the notion that they are somehow making up for the failure of capitalist enterprise to create a more egalitarian society. In fact, the exacerbation of inequality is caused by the central bank in its proactive attempt to micro-manage the natural ebb and flow of economic activity and interfere in the signals contained in market-driven prices (the price of money, i.e. the cost of borrowing in this case) that allow for efficient allocation of savings.

Inherently, in attempting to ensure maximum employment at all times by inflicting a loss of purchasing power on the people, the central banks fail in achieving all of their objectives. The effective loss of purchasing power means money is no longer an actual store of value. As this encourages lax standards in lending and leads to a situation in which asset prices are inadequately supported by wages, it creates a higher risk of instability in the financial system. And as wealth begets wealth faster than labour begets income, the intention of ameliorating social cohesion that underlies the goal of maximum employment is also violated.

Another legacy of the interest rate lever is that those working in the financial services industry – notably the investment banks – earn more than people with similar education and talent who are employed elsewhere. After the financial crisis, the view that investment banks were brutally efficient centres of excellence gave way to aggressive claims that they were unfairly benefiting from an implicit taxpayer guarantee. Almost in answer to the long-standing lament of commentators and academics, remuneration restraints were imposed on the investment banks and other parts of the financial industry. These curbs, though, concealed the dark shadow created by the central banks.

The sales and trading units of investment banks have a business model that is essentially that of a broker bringing buyers and sellers together. Acting as intermediaries, the banks allow their customers to buy or sell financial assets when they want, instead of making them wait until they find someone to do business with. They provide liquidity by allowing the asset owner to sell it for cash and in so doing they take on to their balance sheets (if only for a few minutes, hours and possibly days) the risk that its price may fluctuate. Their commission therefore is more justified than, say, that of a real estate broker who effectively only searches for someone with whom a buyer or seller can transact without taking the risk that the price may move adversely in the interim. And as they take on the risk of asset prices, investment banks can justify charging buyers and sellers a commission.

The remuneration restraints were especially focused on senior management and those engaged in the investment banking roles of sales and trading. The implication was that the banks were engaging in socially useless casino-type gambling, even betting against their own clients – all safe in the knowledge that if things went badly, the government was there to bail them out. But if that was the case, why did independent asset managers – who enjoyed no such support – receive remuneration that was as high or, in some instances, even higher? Were they the most efficient and resourceful pool of workers, or were they also shrewdly exploiting the system? The answer was neither. For the most part they were in the right place at the right time, in a circumstance created by the central banks.

Remember that the value of the stock of financial assets is several times the level of income. In 2013, for instance, US households earned approximately $12.5 trillion in disposable personal income, while the total value of financial assets they held at the end of the year was $65 trillion. This money was invested in cash and money market instruments, as well as various debt and equity investments and included pension entitlements. Other than households and non-profit organisations, there exist corporate institutions (both financial and non-financial by nature) that also own financial assets. Even if the only thing that these owners of financial assets did was to buy their investments and hold on to them, they would nonetheless receive some cash by way of interest, dividends and repayment of principal when bonds matured. This cash then has to be reinvested. In addition, every year households and corporates save a small percentage of their annual income/profits and invest it in various financial assets. All of this is done via an asset manager of some sort, or directly via some internet platform. These intermediaries ultimately go to the investment banks to buy various assets, who then earn a commission on these transactions.

At its most basic, this is the model by which the investment banks operate and earn profits, earning fractions for delivering a service that is driven by the needs of investors who wish to procure investment securities that are issued by governments and corporates, who then use this capital to finance productive economic activity. Developed financial markets are a prerequisite of any large-scale economy to facilitate this movement of savings from saver to user of funds. The pool of global savings then courses through the dealing desks of the investment banks, finally getting invested in various financial assets that then constitute our wealth. As investment returns increase the value of this stock of wealth, the value of the transactions going through the dealing desks also increases, as do the commissions. The greater the number of transactions, the more profits the investment banks can earn. And the more profits they earn, the more they are able to pay themselves – justifiably so, for providing the service of broker and liquidity provider. However, since every transaction is presumably moving money from a saver to a productive user of funds, it has a bigger complement in the real economy. So, even though investment banks are handsomely paid, it only reflects the bigger pie that has come about by virtue of their facilitation.

In the normal course of events, the number of transactions will ebb and flow as investors' needs and perceptions change. However, each time the central banks signal a change in policy to alter asset prices pre-emptively, investors are forced to react and decide what actions are wise, exactly as the central bank wants them to. As a result, the number and type of transactions in the market increase markedly and the dealers earn more commission as a result. When the asset price mechanism fails – which it does, not because there exists a broker, but because the incentives for investors fail to elicit the intended result – the commissions that investment banks earn have no complement in the real economy.

The further that central banks drive yields on risk-free government bonds lower, relative to the perceived strength of the economy, the greater is the incentive for investors to move into riskier investments and to use leverage (by explicitly borrowing to invest more or by buying financial derivatives that effectively do the same) to try to earn higher returns over the cost of borrowing. As risky assets/financial derivatives carry a greater risk of price fluctuations, so the investment banks charge higher commission on these transactions. The greater the demand for these products, the larger the total commission. And these commissions jar ever more relative to the rest of the economy when policy fails to deliver its intended result of engendering productive activity.

So it is not the act of bringing buyers and sellers together and allowing them to transact at the time they wish to (what is referred to as market-making) per se that leads to out-of-the ordinary profits for investment banks. It is only when their broking does not result in productive allocation of savings – something for which the broker does not really carry responsibility, even if they are involved in a fair bit of anticipatory trading and market positioning as a consequence of their market-making. It is only natural to expect the investment banks to provide liquidity without loss-making market exposure, otherwise they would go out of business. Moreover, such behaviour may lead them to make greater profits than if they were strictly hedging every transaction instantaneously, which may not even be possible. Nonetheless, these activities are only marginally additive to market trends generated by savers. Equally, in structuring financial products and selling them on to investors, the investment banks may actually invest in them at the same time, but for the most part they are created to cater to demand from investors. That appetite is not controlled by the investment banks, but determined by incentives generated by risk-free yields on government bonds. Any proprietary position that the investment bank may take is then also in response to the signals that are given by the central bank.

Most asset managers earn a fee that is a percentage of the assets they manage. The service they provide largely centres on selecting the right security and sector within a particular asset class. The manager of a mutual fund that invests in bonds, for instance, will decide which bonds to buy, of what maturity and from which issuer, depending on the constraints imposed by investors. Over time, returns compound and the dollar value of investments grows to compensate for the risk of investment and inflation. However, the further down interest rates go, the greater the value of these investments becomes. And the larger the value, the greater the fee that asset managers earn – again, somewhat independently of their contribution.

All of which is to say that remuneration restraints on those working in investment banks fix a symptom rather than the cause. In the absence of a loss of purchasing power, there would be a natural tendency for savings to chase investments on the strength of their cash flow and their proposed value creation and the saver would be recompensed according to the demand and supply for savings. When people's savings were in excess of investment opportunities, the price of money would fall as if to reflect the slump in activity and vice versa. This would be no more than a reflection of the human tendency to work, then rest, refuel and then work again. In the event that, for some outside reason, the natural ebb and flow was disrupted such that there was a protracted slump in economic activity, there would be a case for the government to avail of a low cost of borrowing to finance economic activity. However, when the central bank tries to act as an employment creator and economic fine-tuner, during a period in which the economy is in a natural period of rest from productive activity, it creates confusion amidst fatigue. In this state of confusion, savers irked by a loss of purchasing power are hustled by the central bank into speculative investments as opposed to the calculated risk-taking of gainful and robust enterprise. It is in this instance that the investment banks' earnings are outsized and without parallel in the wider economy.

Investment banks unwittingly come to earn profits that are outsized relative to the scale of enterprise in the underlying economy, so they naturally attract the best and brightest talent. This compounds the problem of activity without parallel in the real economy, because if a larger than otherwise proportion of the best and brightest end up as mere brokers for enterprise, then enterprise itself is deprived of talent. People with training and aptitude better suited elsewhere succumb to the reality of considerably higher earning potential in the financial sector. They get lured by money and, off-put by lower relative wages outside the financial sector, forego a more inventive, forceful (and in the long run more rewarding in all senses) contribution to society. All because the central banks thought that pre-emptively boosting capital asset prices by way of negative real interest rates was the key to unleashing human ingenuity.

19

The Veil of Price Stability

Depending on who you ask, the prospect of inflation gets a mixed reaction. If you're on a fixed salary with little scope to negotiate your wages, then inflation is fairly unwelcome. The same can be said for creditors who lend their hard-earned savings: any inflation they didn't factor in leaves them undercompensated. But if you're a debtor, paying a fixed rate of interest that does not fully reflect the effective rate of inflation, it is a good thing. Especially when property funded by debt is increasing in value at a rate that overcompensates for inflation.

But despite this redistribution between debtors and capital asset owners on one side, and creditors and fixed wage earners on the other, inflation appears to have some serious benefits. Consider a business owner or entrepreneur who takes out a loan and fixes the interest rate for the next two years, but then over time there is more inflation than initially expected and so the price at which he sells his goods rises. Not only does inflation reduce the real burden of his debt, he also earns more revenue than he had previously thought feasible. And as there is a surplus of people looking for work, which allows existing employees little wage negotiability, he benefits further as he is able to retain them without having to adjust their wages higher to fully compensate for inflation. With revenues adjusting upwards, while interest and wage costs stay the same, his profits increase and on this basis he decides to expand production.

Given all this, one could reasonably ask why unanticipated inflation is considered a bad thing. The person earning a fixed wage must be glad that he has any wage at all: without the profits that his boss gained because of inflation he might not have a job. The undercompensated lender, meanwhile, must be glad to have his money back with some amount of return, even if he was not adequately compensated for all the risks of inflation, growth and potential default. And besides, at the rate that he may feel fully compensated, the borrower may not have been able to afford the loan at all. So while the lender may not have got his full due, the chances of him actually getting that had little prospect of ever coming good.

But sooner or later wage earners and creditors realise that prices have risen and demand compensation. Jobs are more plentiful now so the business owner cannot retain workers by paying effectively lower real wages and at the next re-fixing the lender raises the cost of borrowing. As our business owner is convinced that he can get still higher prices for his product, he pays the higher costs and continues expansion. And for these purposes he borrows further.

So long as prices keep rising faster than the adjustment of real wages and his interest costs, our business owner, alongside others like him in the economy, participates in an inflationary boom. However, as wage earners and creditors realise that they are being systematically unfairly compensated, they start to demand ever-increasing compensation. Once wages and interest costs have fully adjusted higher in real terms, the profits on which businesses based their decision to expand suddenly disappear. They realise that what they had mistakenly thought was relative demand for their products was actually just inflation, which is now reflected in the price of goods and services, labour and money. Yet, supply and indebtedness have meanwhile increased considerably in response to perceived higher relative demand. Without the demand they had anticipated for their goods, a great many businesses find themselves facing losses. As they retrench, the apparent boom that inflation had created suddenly gives way to bust – inventory lies unsold, workers are laid off, demand falls further and bad debts are everywhere. All that unanticipated inflation did was to create a false signal of higher profits and relative demand that confused people into over-extending production and misallocating capital. An eventual spike higher in real wages and/or interest rates finally precipitated the bust.

So while a gradual effective loss of purchasing power may be beneficial for governments and businesses as it reduces the real burden of their debt and wage costs, an increase in expectations of yet higher rates of inflation becomes counterproductive, as it risks rendering employees and lenders less acquiescent while giving businesses an inaccurate indication of relative demand.

This is why central banks are very keen on preventing a rise in inflation expectations. To this extent, the central banks seem to have done a splendid job. Almost all measures of consumer price inflation for goods and services have been close to 2 per cent in the US and the UK for much of the last two decades. The constancy of this number has anchored expectations and made for a more amenable public, so much so that the central banks have been able to sanctify the 2 per cent level as a 'good thing' in itself. And this has allowed them to engineer a systematic loss of purchasing power, as and when needed to reduce real debt burdens and aid profitability, even while avoiding the downside of rising inflation expectations.

But before congratulating the central banks on having so effectively performed this sleight of hand, notice the pattern in asset prices since the late 1990s. A drop in long-term risk-free interest rates triggers a disproportional rise in the price of risky assets. Everyone who holds them feels that much richer: a feel-good factor of wealth and prosperity arrives. However, this also creates expectations of further price rises, so investors borrow to invest more so they can enjoy higher returns. So long as risky asset prices are rising more than borrowing costs, the asset boom keeps going. Soon, investors start to sell risk-free bonds to invest yet further in risky assets. The boom continues despite the rise in risk-free rates, so long as risk premiums demanded by investors go lower at the same time. However, the higher risk-free yields go, the less inclined investors are to accept less compensation for extra risk. As they raise the compensation they require, borrowing costs increase and risky assets fall. And money borrowed to finance these purchases suddenly turns to bad debt, which leads to a further spike in borrowing costs. All that the initial disproportional jump in asset prices had done was to create confusion as to the real value of these assets and led investors to over-leverage by borrowing too much against them. The boom lasted until borrowing costs were contained either because risk-free rates or investor risk premiums or both stayed low. No sooner had either spiked higher, than the boom turned to bust.

The seeming anchoring of inflation expectations at 2 per cent merely acts as a veil. The confusion unleashed by spiralling expectations of further price rises and the misallocation of capital that results from it merely play out in asset markets as opposed to the market of consumer goods and services. So while central banks can congratulate themselves on delivering stable consumer price inflation at 2 per cent, the instability elsewhere renders it a meaningless feat.

20

Trading Versus Investing

N ewton's first law of motion states that an object will remain at rest or in uniform motion in a straight line unless it is acted upon by an external force. Apply this law to the overall stock, real estate or fixed-income markets and you can draw a similar conclusion. If the pay-out from an asset and the interest rate are known and fixed, then we can arrive at the asset's present value. The value of the asset in question would be fixed – effectively in a state of rest. Pay-outs in the form of rental income, dividends and interest income, however, are changing over time in proportion to the strength of the underlying economy, as is the interest rate which fluctuates to reflect growth. The price of the asset is therefore in motion and will remain so, moving at a 'velocity' close to that of the economy.

Human emotion acts as an external force upon this trend velocity. Financial panics therefore risk dislodging asset prices and the economy from their trend. So there is a valid role for the central bank to counterbalance these forces by lowering risk-free interest rates to mitigate the impact of starkly higher risk premiums demanded by panicked investors and lenders. However, when the central banks treat asset markets as conduits for economic growth, they apply an external force that does not just counterbalance. They effectively reinforce positive human emotion and the inclination to borrow and lend, which greatly accelerates the velocity of the asset price, making it move much faster than the underlying real economy.

When the stock market fell in September and October 1998 – as investors panicked after Russia's debt default and the bailout of LTCM – the central banks lowered rates to induce investors to lower their risk premium for investing in risky assets. The move worked: the stock market had recovered all its hefty losses by the end of the year, and corporates were even showing a tendency towards excess. But by keeping rates low when investors' sentiment had already turned so forcefully, the central banks started to add to positive human emotion from that point on – knowingly so, as they thought it would lead to greater growth. Similarly, when the Bank of England cut its interest rates in 2001 and the economy started booming by early 2002, by not reversing its rate cuts the Bank significantly enhanced the feel-good factor fuelling the housing market and, consequently, levels of debt.

By repeatedly acting as an additional external force on asset prices, the central banks change the very nature of investing. It ceases to be a simple case of buying and holding investments that relies on the fact that the stock market as a whole or house prices will follow the economy as it grows, over time. In that case, we can choose to ignore a certain amount of volatility that comes with the normal ebb and flow of human emotion. We may be reassured that, over the long term, asset markets will eventually gravitate to where the economy moves as a result of its labour, capital, technological progress, the soundness of its financial institutions and the competency of its government.

However, when the central banks actively reinforce positive human emotion and the supply of credit, asset prices exhibit magnified herd behaviour, much like the seasonal migration of animals through the Serengeti and Masai Mara regions in Africa. There is, however, no such seasonal predictability to how far the central banks will go, given that their gauge of consumer price inflation is rendered ineffective by the inadequate equalisation of relative demand for capital assets and consumer goods and services. So investors are forced to be vigilant, nervously peering through clouds of dust kicked up by the thundering herd of investors, trying to ascertain if there is danger of sudden collapse from a rise in risk-free yields and/or investor risk premiums.

Great asset trends triggered by central banks, together with the nervous jockeying that becomes necessary on the part of the investor, naturally create their own winners and losers. They favour active traders and hedge fund managers who aim to extract value by anticipating the actions of the central banks. Also, index tracker funds or exchange-traded funds, as they are referred to, become the cost-effective choice for investors to gain exposure to the currently popular asset class (or sector within it) that is effectively serving as the central banks' conduit. Investment funds that traditionally aimed at beating the market by selecting securities and sectors (or mutual funds as they are more often called) become a harder sell to investors, in what is a synchronised move aided by the central banks. If they thrive it is more due to the pull of star managers, brand safety and competitive pricing, than their ability to make a meaningful difference by selecting sectors and securities.

The game of bluff elevates speculation to an economic necessity and disrupts the efficient allocation of capital. It has relegated to antiquity the type of investing that involves buying and holding of carefully selected, value-generating investments over the long term. The key decision for investors is which asset class to invest in and when. This is a direct result of the interest rate lever, which, by force of its disproportionate impact on asset prices and coercive loss of purchasing power, dominates all other factors. The specifics of a firm or investment matter far less if the entire stock or corporate bond market becomes attractive because of a drop in risk-free interest rates. Anticipating the central bank becomes vital as negative real risk-free rates have the potential to make risky assets surge in the short term, independently of long-term growth prospects.

However, for this very reason, these asset price trends are susceptible to sudden death when investors collectively raise their risk premiums upon being faced with the economic reality. Over time, a buy and hold investor can live through episodes in which their investments fall by 5 to 10 per cent in the short term. But drops of 20 or 30 per cent or more make buy and hold approaches impractical. There are investors with deep pockets for whom the investment time horizon is very long term – twenty to thirty years or more, as for pension and sovereign wealth funds. However, even if they can ignore the dramatic rises and falls in entire asset classes over relatively short periods, they recognise an opportunity that can be exploited. This is why most supposed long-term investors focus on short-term asset-allocation trades, and choose to outsource them to hedge funds that specialise in extracting value by aggressively trading these exaggerated trends and consequent corrections in asset prices over the short term.

Capital-rich, would-be entrepreneurs may well ask themselves if the messy effort of setting up business is worthwhile when they can invest in a liquid stock market or a hedge fund that exploits large trends in financial markets, and potentially make 20 to 30 per cent returns in a year. The central banks' use of asset prices therefore creates a paradoxical situation in which savings are less likely to be channelled into creating value. If asset wealth that results from liquid investing is then not monetised into greater spending by whoever it enriches, then the impact on the real economy of setting up business and investing in the stock market or a hedge fund is not the same. This only widens the gap between the asset economy and the rest of the economy and obliges the central bank to stay involved in supporting it.

In light of the financial market volatility that results from the central banks' game of bluff, the classic 'invest don't trade' advice rings hollow – exposed by the other cliché 'a long-term investment is simply a short-term trade gone wrong'. Those who take the stance that trading is a socially useless activity compared with investing are wilfully blind to the fact that the speculative motive is fanned and exploited by the central banks, in an attempt to create economic growth. It's only when the bluff is exposed that the policy makers cry foul.

21

Under the Hood

Joe and John are two brothers, both with the requisite drive and business acumen to succeed. John, the elder brother, is steady, hard-working and cautious. So when his younger brother calls to tell him he's got a job offer and the pay looks great, John's immediate response is, 'That sounds good. But did you look under the hood?'

'What do you mean?' replies Joe, a little puzzled.

'Well, if you were buying a used car, you'd need to look for loose wires hidden under the shiny bonnet that may cost you a lot in hassle and repairs just when you need a dependable ride. Did the boss-to-be look like he was just in it for himself, or was he going to watch out for his team and give you room to grow? Does he look like he could be rash and mercurial – anything that might mean that you're better off waiting for other opportunities?'

Joe thinks to himself, 'As far as I can see, my prospective boss makes a ton of money, looks really confident and in control. I feel privileged to be joining his team. Besides, they're offering me a whopping 200 grand a year. This other offer I had pays 55k and my big brother who's really smart and hard-working only makes 60k. I think this is the real deal.'

Joe accepts the offer and works really long hours, putting into practice all the good work ethics his big brother has taught him. But it turns out his confident and in-control boss makes a series of bad decisions, landing his division with a big loss within a year of Joe's joining. The firm sacks the boss and Joe, who is seen as his protégé, also gets the push. In the meantime, the economy has turned: Joe is out of a job just when everyone else is also laying off workers. His hard-working brother, meanwhile, has been promoted and his salary has doubled to $120,000 a year.

Much like Joe's fate, all the while that investors are being impressed by the central banks' bluster of cheap money, there is a dynamic under way that makes long-term prospects less stable. Lower borrowing costs enable companies to increase leverage by issuing debt to then buy back their stock in the market with the cash. The resulting boost to the stock market is significant and acts to bamboozle the investor yet further.

Let's say a company has issued 100 million shares that are trading at $100 per share, making it worth $10 billion. It earns $600 million a year, which effectively means $6 of earnings per share. If the company raises $2.4 billion of debt at, say, 2 per cent for five years ($48 million interest per year) to buy back 24 million shares in the market, it raises its earnings by 21 per cent to $7 per share,[1] all else being equal. As long as earnings stay stable or keep rising to compensate for the debt servicing cost, the remaining shareholders have substantially more earnings, for which investors are ready to pay more.

The boost to the stock market that comes from the buyback of shares by companies availing themselves of cheap borrowing costs acts to validate the central banks' bluff in the eyes of the investors. As they are lulled into reducing their risk premium further and buying more forcefully, company managements in turn feel validated in their actions. They are more likely to interpret stock price gains as an affirmation of their skills in steering company strategy. As they become more confident of future earnings, they are encouraged to leverage further.

Leverage, however, becomes an issue if companies' earnings are hit by an economic slowdown that leaves them with falling revenue receipts in the face of a fixed cost of furnishing debt. Worse still, if in the wake of falling revenues, borrowing costs rise. (In our example, a 30 per cent fall in earnings from $600 million to $420 million a year alongside a doubling of borrowing costs to 4 per cent per year or $96 million makes the earnings per share drop to $4.)

An even worse situation arises if lenders shy away altogether such that they are unable to rollover their debts. Companies then have to expedite asset sales, even as markets are falling, to raise cash to pay off their existing debts. Or they can reissue shares, which magnifies the decrease in earnings per share. Under the hood of the reflation and recovery engineered by the central bank is the inevitable rise in risk that comes with greater debt. The fixed costs of furnishing debt raise the stakes for shareholders as there is a bigger pot to be shared by a fewer number. However, on the downside it makes them vulnerable to a downturn in which its creditors may become more demanding or vanish altogether.

In the last two quarters of 1998 in the US, as rates went down and the stock market corrected, non-financial corporations came out in droves to buy their own stock.[2] If the Fed was

195

worried about negative sentiment in the economy, it certainly wasn't a mood shared by these companies: the fact that they were taking on debt to buy back their own equities meant that they expected things to get better not worse. After rates were held low in the first half of 1999, non-financial corporations issued debt with gusto. Although as stock prices started to rise they slowed down their buybacks in tandem. By 2000, non-financial corporates had significantly increased leverage, which made them vulnerable to a rise in interest rates. In the years that followed, debt issuance and buybacks almost stopped. The fact that the stock market posted a couple of years of negative returns was no surprise.

By 2005, debt issuance and buybacks had started anew. In 2007, corporates were issuing debt and buying back their shares at a rate several times faster than usual. By 2008, the bloat was looking very similar to that in 2000. Low borrowing costs relative to the growth of the economy had been fertile ground for leveraging. But then the credit crunch hit, and these companies were forced not only to ease the pace of their leveraging, but also to reduce the size of their debt. This repair mode, however, only lasted a short time. The central banks engineered low interest rates once more, and by 2011 the debt bloat had started again and was once more being used to fund buybacks. By 2013, investors had noticed that the stock market had recovered and that cash-equivalent investments were yielding returns much below inflation. The result was a stellar year for the equity markets, which were buoyed by debt-funded buybacks and investors lured back to riskier assets.

By the end of 2015, indebtedness in non-financial corporate America (as a proportion of the rest of the economy) was close to the precarious levels seen in 2000 and 2007. Whether the leveraging of corporate America (non-financial companies) proves to be a destabilising factor for the US economy yet again will depend on the generosity of lenders in relation to how fast their earnings grow. It is a precarious balancing act that no doubt the Fed will try to manage. The fact that corporate America has chosen a riskier route with less room for error, and so soon after the crises of 2000–02 and 2007–09, is testament to the power of the Fed's coercive bluff of 'low for long' interest rates, and its implicit promise of prosperity. One can only hope that equity investors look under the hood, though this may be too much to ask of them. Sub-inflation compensation on government bonds and their savings accounts may prove precisely the sort of temptation that the central banks hope they will fall for.

22

The Bubble That Never Burst

If you are a long-term Londoner, chances are that you know at least one very miserable and unhappy person who fought the meteoric rise in house prices since the late 1990s, swearing they weren't going to be the fool who bought at the top of the market and was holding out for the crash instead. Except when the crash in London house prices did come to pass, it was so shallow and fleeting that it may as well have never happened in the first place. If only your frustrated friend had known that they were up against a systematic and synchronised policy of cheap money by the lead central banks of the West, they could have been spared a fair bit of misery.

The central banks had been focused on keeping consumer price inflation low. Whether intentionally or unintentionally, this had them looking left when the train was coming from the right. Excess money in the economy was finding its way into assets that offered the best insurance against a stealth inflationary bias. If the central banks were to be trusted and protection was not needed against any intentional bias, then chasing capital assets was nonetheless justified as insurance against superfluous money that escaped their attention. There was certainly plenty of money around, as even a casual look at the global financial and property markets would have revealed.

In the ten years of the Bank of England's independence, the London housing[1] market had trebled. It had already secured its place alongside the other great property bubbles in the US and Japan. From 1981 to 1991, land prices in Japan's three major cities[2] had also trebled, although admittedly most of that rise had come in the preceding five years. House prices in ten major US cities,[3] meanwhile, rose by a factor of 2.9 over 1997 and 2006, not far behind the property booms in London and Japan.

By the end of 2015, however, land prices in Japan were 65 per cent lower than they had been at their peak, while house prices in the ten major US cities lost one-third of their value from the highs, over a protracted period of five years. London, however, proved to be an outlier as it brushed off a correction like a seasonal cold. Prices dipped by about 15 per cent over a year from mid-2008, but by mid-2009 were once again on the ascent. By the end of 2015, house prices had risen by almost 50 per cent more than their value at the pre-crisis peak: the trebling experienced in the first ten years of the Bank of England's independence was now over a quadrupling. Prices in the rest of England and Wales, by contrast, experienced a similar fall in value between 2008 and 2009, but were then slower to recover to their pre-crisis peak. By the end of 2015, they had just about recovered to their pre-crisis peak.

From the point of view of rectifying the aftermath of ten years of cheap money – if not in absolute terms then at least in relation to the economy – the Bank of England went on to almost pull off a coup in the post-crisis period. There is no better cure for a heavy debt load than inflation. As the Bank of England had been pushing what was effectively a higher inflation rate in the services sector, masked by justified deflation in the price of goods, the economy found it psychologically less crippling, especially with interest rates at near zero. Nevertheless, growth in household borrowing slowed dramatically, non-financial companies pared down their debt, and the banking sector reined in its leverage. All this while the economy had grown by a cumulative 22 per cent over the five years from 2010 to 2014, a significant proportion of which was simply inflation.

Escalating house prices in London had, however, become a very significant and visible issue, given that these rises were well in excess of wage growth. The Bank attempted to deflect attention away from this, pointing to the fact that household debt was no longer growing while the rest of the economy was – London indeed accounted for less than one-fifth of Britain's total household income.[4] It pointed out that it was obliged to look at the rest of the UK, where house prices were not rising by as much. It argued that Russians and Europeans were fleeing political and economic instability and parking money in prime London real estate, a factor outside its control. Finally, it trotted out the age-old excuse that had led everyone down the perilous journey of the ten years between 1997 and 2007: consumer price inflation was not an issue and would fall to targeted levels sooner or later. Given that consumer prices were relatively contained, the Bank was more worried about those who were unemployed and at risk of losing their skills from disuse.

To some extent all these factors were indeed true. Yet the Bank ignored all the warning signs of inherent instability and crises to come that had been flashing in the pre-crisis period.

The pattern of monetary excess being funnelled into certain pockets of assets was once again playing out in London house prices. While the prices of consumer goods and services were not rising in a similar way, London house prices were caught in their own inflationary tornado, sucking in capital and creating a self-fulfilling expectation of further rises.

Until 2007, the upscale boroughs had risen at the same rate as the rest of greater London. Now prices in the most expensive boroughs of Kensington and Chelsea, and Westminster, broke away from the rest of London's other thirty-one boroughs by virtue of international demand for prime real estate. They rose by as much as 65 per cent from their pre-crisis peaks to the end of 2015, effectively quintupling in value since December 1997, compared with the four-fold increase across London as a whole.

While foreign demand explained the upward trend in super-prime real estate, it was not a satisfactory reason for the giddying rise in other parts of London. The more accurate explanation for this was that the surfeit of money generated by the Bank of England was being funnelled into London real estate. As for the Bank of England's policy of super-cheap money far beyond the panic period of 2007–09, as well as the government's mortgage subsidy scheme, the question that arose was this: why were they so intent on jointly inflating unsustainable house prices in Britain when they should have been focusing on getting incomes to catch up? Furthermore, the Bank had no answers to the question of how it was going to solve the problem it was creating by relying on the asset price mechanism of low interest rates, which was effectively exacerbating the gap between incomes and assets once more, even if overall debt as a proportion of income was coming down.

Affordability of housing mattered just as much, if not more, to social cohesion than getting people jobs. As hard as people worked, they seemed ever further away from owning a home within a reasonably long commute from work. The government's mortgage subsidy schemes compounded the problem created by the Bank's broken cheap money policy. By supporting unsustainable house prices, it was merely adding to the taxpayer's burden further down the road.

The unsustainability of Britain's housing market was evident in the price to earnings gap. The ratio of median house prices to earnings[5] in England in 2013 was 6.72, about half a point lower than its peak in 2010 – though it had been just 3.5 in 1997. The same ratio for the fourteen boroughs of inner[6] London had risen steadily to a little over ten – median house prices were ten times earnings. It clearly demonstrated what the vast majority was up against.

Inferring rental income from gross earnings by making an assumption that people pay 20 per cent of income as taxes and then spend a quarter of their net income on rent reveals that it would take roughly fifty-two years[7] to pay off the purchase price of a London house. For England as a whole, if one assumed that people paid only one-fifth of their income after tax on rent, it would take forty-two years[8] to pay off the property. Back in 1997, the equivalent figure was just twenty-two years. This shows the extent to which house prices were propelled upwards and sustained by low interest rates and a rise in debt.

The concentration of wealth belonging to the world's richest people in two of London's most upscale neighbourhoods captures a lot of attention. But it obscures a second, much larger, fallout: the pressure that young Londoners feel as a result of an ever-widening gap between house prices and income. It is a divide that suckers them into buying property at an early stage in their lives. It is also a divide that monetary policy is blind to, and relies on a mechanism to rectify it – a mechanism that has failed in the previous two decades and caused the problem in the first place. People in the 21–30 age bracket see purchasing property as their main goal, which, family largesse aside, they can only achieve by acquiring a millstone of debt. At a time in their careers when they should be taking the maximum chances, unsaddled by debt, to secure jobs that allow them to achieve their full potential, their focus instead is on getting on to the property ladder. Sadly, the probability of a 'snakes and ladders' outcome is high: a climb towards the top only to find that markets crash and they end up with a move back down to the bottom again.

The divide between house prices and income is seen to be the result of a supply shortage. There is little awareness that it is the result of a failed bluff, a malfunction of monetary policy – one that has caused a surfeit of cheap money to funnel into an asset class without the intended follow through of proportional demand for wider consumer goods and services and wages. Inflationary expectations have been channelled into higher house prices, rather than the prices of consumer goods and services. This inflation confuses the picture, so it isn't clear which portion of demand is generated by inflationary expectations and which caused by a real shortage. It goes without saying that anything that goes up in price by double digits annually will create so much demand in itself that even otherwise ample supply relative to real housing needs will be rendered inadequate! Especially when that demand is financed by paper money, which in principle is infinite. The misallocation of capital that results from the confusion about what is sustainable demand and what is the result of superfluous money is the typical consequence of high inflation that textbooks warn us about.

The diagnosis that house price rises are due to a supply shortage has led to rallying calls for more houses. However, if there was such an imbalance in supply and demand, the question was why supply wasn't catching up with this juicy demand. It was more likely that suppliers had a better understanding of the price–income divide, and were wary of building more houses when people had limited ability to buy at the prices they were willing to sell at. But construction also comes with a considerable time lag. So, it may well be possible that there is supply in the pipeline, on the basis that sellers imagine prices will continue to rise at the same pace. However, a surfeit of houses on the market – unimaginable as it may sound – must cap selling prices, especially if interest rates have risen in the meantime. As for buyers, they may find that they only wanted an asset that they thought was going to rise forever, rather than one that suddenly sits heavily in the market. A surge in supply coupled with a rise in borrowing costs is a recipe for a spectacular bust, especially when the asset is financed by debt.

A positive outcome can prevail only if wages and rents rise even when borrowing costs are increasing such that house prices do not rise in tandem. However, should the gulf between house prices and earnings remain and more housing stock come on to the market, it can either be sold to foreign buyers or result in an increase in debt relative to income. Neither of these options is desirable: the first leaves housing outside the reach of local residents, and the second makes the economy and banks more debt-laden and therefore vulnerable to a change in credit and economic conditions. If neither of these options transpires, builders are left with the problem that there are no buyers willing to pay the price they want to sell at.

Barring an ever-growing flow of foreign buyers or another explosion of debt, it is not unreasonable to expect that any increase in supply will be met with a considerable and protracted drop in prices. The tricky question is what the Bank of England would do in this instance. Banks will no doubt come under stress, as homeowners find themselves in negative equity and a recessionary dynamic unfolds. Would the Bank drop interest rates more, inflating and taxing savers so that house prices stay at their unsustainable levels? How much would they have to inflate, and what would be the unintended consequences? Whatever these consequences might be, fatigue at yet another asset price-led bust will surely reign supreme.

23

Gold Glitter

Soon after the temporary suspension of gold payments against the dollar in March 1933, the US government announced its intention to devalue the dollar in an attempt to reflate prices and ease the stranglehold of debt deflation that had asphyxiated business. The Gold Reserve Act, passed in January 1934, marked a return to convertibility of the US dollar but devalued it to 59 per cent of its former weight in gold – the price of a troy ounce of gold went from $20.67 before the announcement to being fixed at $35, once the Act was passed.

The currency system that emerged after the Second World War was effectively one in which the dollar was pegged to gold at $35 per troy ounce, with the other major currencies fixed against the US currency. However, the US government's inflationary bias, supported by the premise that there existed a positive trade-off between inflation and unemployment, would soon make the peg to gold unsustainable. As other governments justifiably sold the surfeit of dollars to buy gold from the US, in August 1971 President Richard Nixon decided to suspend convertibility of the dollar to gold altogether.

US consumer price inflation had been running at about 5 per cent per year since the late 1960s, but given the peg to gold, oil prices – which were quoted in US dollars – had remained stable. With the unpegging of the dollar it was only a matter of time before oil prices were revalued upwards. The dollar price of oil adjusted sharply upwards against the backdrop of the Arab-Israeli hostilities in 1973 and 1974. Together with the psychological effects of a government unfettered by the constraint of its gold reserves, this unleashed an upward spiral in inflationary expectations. By December 1974, US consumer prices were rising at a rate of 12 per cent a year. By the end of 1976 inflation had dropped back to 5 per cent, before rising to a rate of almost 15 per cent per year as oil prices spiked higher after the Iranian revolution in 1979.

Following the unpegging of the dollar, the rising dollar price of gold epitomised the loss of confidence in the dollar as a store of value. At the end of December 1980, the price of a troy ounce closed at $590, after overshooting to as much as $850 earlier that year from its peg of $35 a decade earlier. Consumer prices in the US had slightly more than doubled in the preceding ten years, but the value of gold had risen by more than seventeen times. In the 1980s and 1990s, gold and consumer prices moved more in line with one another. By December 1999, the price of gold had almost halved to $288 per troy ounce, while consumer prices had again doubled. With central banks committed to targeting inflation at 2 per cent a year, the premium value of gold as insurance against unanticipated inflation gradually dissipated. By the end of the 1990s, the role of gold in international markets seemed to have become an anachronism.

Then, suddenly, the dynamics changed. In 2002, gold prices started to move steadily higher, even while consumer price inflation remained close to 2 per cent, and the central banks were lowering interest rates to combat the supposed deflationary aftermath of a collapse in asset prices. By the end of 2007, gold had tripled in price to $834 per ounce, an increase of 200 per cent during the six years since 2001. The shift was much greater than either the depreciation of the dollar, which had fallen by roughly one-third against other major currencies, or the rise in US consumer prices, which cumulatively had risen by 19 per cent in the same period. The measure for consumer price inflation that the Fed looks at – price index for personal consumption expenditures – averaged a little over 2 per cent per year during this period and other market indicators for inflation expectations were also anchored close by.

Why was it, then, that the price of gold was overcompensating so dramatically, just as it had in the 1970s, when all measures of consumer prices had been rising at double-digit rates? The simplest answer is that the dollar price of gold was reflective of the dichotomy of asset and consumer prices and was adjusting to capture the full inflationary impetus that was funnelling into the former, as opposed to simply reflecting money that was chasing consumer goods and services.

There was a coincident surge in oil prices, which had risen by almost five times during the six years to the end of 2007. Whether this was the result of genuine excess world demand relative to supply or was also a recipient of superfluous dollars, alongside other assets, as a better store of value cannot be ascertained for sure. A marked increase in oil production in the US came in answer to the upsurge in the oil price. However, a perceived glut from excess supply saw the price of oil lose almost two-thirds of its value over 2014 and 2015. It is arguable that the oil price swings were the result of the confusion that results from superfluous money, misleading producers by giving incorrect signals of relative demand.

At the end of 2015, the dollar price of gold was 45 per cent lower than its high in 2011, having fallen substantially in anticipation of an end to the Fed's monetary easing. However, at $1,061 per troy ounce, it was still almost four times (or 300 per cent higher) where it had been at the end of 2001. In comparison, prices for US consumer goods and services over the entire fourteen-year period from 2001 to 2015 had cumulatively risen 34 per cent.

Going forward, this disconnect between gold and consumer price trends is likely to remain symptomatic of the malfunction of monetary policy, either as a barometer of superfluous money that remains choked in the asset economy or conversely as a portent of a deflationary asset bust as a consequence of rising interest rates or lower appetite for risk on the part of investors.

24

Infantry in the Line of Bluff

The opening line of a brief summary of the Dodd-Frank Wall Street reform and consumer protection Act – 'Years without accountability for Wall Street and big banks brought us the worst financial crisis since the Great Depression, the loss of 8 million jobs, failed businesses, a drop in housing prices, and wiped out personal savings'[1] – provides the reasoning behind what is considered to be the biggest overhaul of the US banking system since the Great Depression.

The genesis of the Act lay in the collapse of Lehman Brothers, an investment bank that failed because it took too much risk in proportion to its capital, and was unable to raise the necessary cash to fulfil its commitments. In an economy where investments were turning sour, no one would lend it any money because there were questions about the quality of its collateral. The failure of Lehman Brothers threw up the same issues as the crises involving Overend, Gurney and Co. and Barings Bank in the latter half of the 1800s. As with Barings, saving Lehman's required a leap of faith by backers with financial heft, because the consequences of not doing so were profound. And as with

Overend, Gurney and Co., Lehman Brothers was up to its neck in the excesses of the day and its collapse unleashed a panic unequalled in recent financial history, which cost more to fix than it would have to save the company in the first place.

At the core of the Dodd-Frank Act was a move to rectify the 'too big to fail' issue surrounding large financial institutions that forces taxpayers to bail them out. The scale and interconnectedness of banks today threatens to wreak havoc on the rest of the economy, making a bailout imperative. The idea therefore is to do away with the need for bailing out large and complex financial companies by requiring them to submit plans of how they may be unwound by the Federal Deposit Insurance Company (FDIC) in the event of bankruptcy. All losses would then be borne by the shareholders and unsecured creditors as opposed to the taxpayer. With the aim of safeguarding taxpayers, the FDIC will only be able to borrow funds that can be repaid through the liquidation of a bankrupt company's assets. It may still guarantee the debt of solvent insured banks to prevent bank runs, but with significant administrative roadblocks. Such guarantees would require a majority of the FDIC and Federal Reserve Board to agree that there was indeed a threat to financial stability, and also for the US Treasury and Congress to approve the terms and conditions. The Act also places limits on the Fed's authority to give out emergency loans to prohibit bailouts of individual companies. The Fed cannot lend to a failing financial firm; any loans would have to be approved by the Treasury, and require sufficient collateral to protect taxpayers from losses.

The Act established a Financial Stability Oversight Council (FSOC), as well as an Office of Financial Research, to collect and analyse data to identify and monitor systemic risk – a build-up of risk exposure in financial institutions that could in aggregate deeply destabilise the economy. On the basis of its assessment, the Council can recommend that the Fed make capital, leverage, liquidity and risk management provisions for banks and financial companies more stringent. And should it feel that a particular financial institution poses too large a threat to the economy as a result of its size, risk-taking and interconnectedness with other banks and non-bank firms, it can then spearhead its break-up. The Fed is tasked with carrying out an annual stress test of all the large bank holding companies and other financial firms designated by the FSOC. The idea behind these stress tests is to evaluate whether financial institutions have the requisite capital to absorb economic and trading losses in adverse situations. So if a sequence of events similar to those that happened after the collapse of Lehman Brothers were to occur, the tests would reveal whether these institutions have the wherewithal to survive without requiring taxpayers' money.

The Act didn't stop at crash-testing the banks and making fold-up provisions. It also prohibited the alleged trading cesspits that used banks' capital to make casino-style bets on asset prices under the banner of proprietary trading. Neither could banks sponsor hedge funds and private equity firms that effectively did the same but with investors' money. Hedge funds and private equity firms did not escape either. They are now required to register with the Securities and Exchange Commission (SEC) as investment advisors, and are also required to divulge information about their trades and portfolios – again so that any build-up of systemic risk can be gauged by the FSOC.

Further, it allows for the clawback of bonuses – publicly traded companies can take back incentive compensation if it

213

transpires that executives have lied about their financial figures. Mortgage reform introduced to promote responsible lending requires lenders to ensure that borrowers can repay, and there are penalties for irresponsible lending. The Act also makes other stipulations for protection of consumers and investors, and for greater transparency and accountability of derivative instruments. Notable among these are various provisions for central clearing and exchange trading for standardised derivatives, regulation of over-the-counter derivatives by the SEC and the Commodity Futures Trading Commission, and the establishment of an Office of Credit Ratings at the SEC to monitor and regulate credit rating agencies.

For all the bombastic breadth of the Dodd-Frank Act, it is what those who conceived it missed that will eventually prove that it did little to truly overhaul the system. They missed the nature of a financial panic, confused correlation with causality and tried to fix the problem by addressing the symptoms one by one, when the inherent cause lay untrammelled.

The crisis of 2007–09 did not happen because financial institutions had become too big. It was caused by a panic that left financial institutions unable to offload their assets for cash or use them as collateral for loans. There were no financial derivatives at the time of Overend, Gurney and Co. and Barings, and the City of London – while not small – had a scale far smaller than that of US financial markets today. Yet the same dynamic occurred, with predictable consequences. Even the run-up to the events was similar: a central bank hesitant to make a loan on grounds of insufficient collateral in an economic climate when many investments were turning sour, and unable to secure the necessary backing of Parliament in case the assets did turn out to be worthless.

A financial panic occurs because of a loss of confidence; the very fact that a financial institution has folded, in however orderly a fashion, can be enough to spark that loss of confidence. The fractional reserve feature of banking renders it susceptible to a panic in which otherwise high levels of capital can prove inadequate. Of course, it helps to have more capital and to have taken less risk in the first place. But taking risks in itself is not an issue: the same panic could have occurred with half the level of risk-taking relative to the amount of loss-absorbing capital held by institutions. A panic marks down otherwise sound investments because it causes banks and investors to sell assets en masse to obtain cash, rendering bad what was otherwise good. As this happens, asset prices decline, loans are recalled and businesses are forced to retrench: the results validate the panic.

The Dodd-Frank summary – which essentially says that the big banks caused businesses to fail, house prices to fall and savings to be wiped out – can just as well be inverted. The reason that banks failed in the first place was because house prices fell, businesses failed and savings were wiped out, so that banks' assets no longer had the value that had been attributed to them earlier. It is not because of the banks that house prices fell, financial markets crashed and jobs were lost. That all of these things are correlated and tend to occur at the same time does not prove one-way causality.

House prices and financial assets crashed because central banks used the interest rate lever to pre-emptively pump their values in the expectation that this would then trigger greater spending and further formation of capital assets such that demand for consumer goods and services and wages would proportionately rise. It was a bluff that belies monetary policy, and not a fool-proof mechanism that results in a stable outcome. The proactive provisioning of reserves to the commercial banks and negative real interest rates by no means guarantees a higher income stream. Moreover, had commercial banks and investors not lowered their credit standards and risk premiums as they did, the Fed would have turned ever more coercive, up until the point that they did as they were expected to. But then when rates were raised, losses stacked up because borrowers who were supposed to have been earning more as a result of the boom engineered by the central bank were unable to service their debts. So lenders legitimately demanded higher rates to compensate them for the risk of lending, as did investors on all risky assets. As asset prices fell, it weighed on business and consumer confidence, damaging the banks' asset base most of all. This made them more reluctant to lend and credit became scarce, amplifying the economic contraction. If investors shied away from buying mortgage-backed securities in the wake of mortgage defaults by US homeowners, the banks had little say in the matter. If the fear of further losses forced investors to walk away from equities and corporate debt, again this had little to do with the banks – even if they had also rightfully ceased their lines of credit to businesses at the same time.

As far back as 1793, the loss of confidence among lenders proved that a credit crunch could only effectively be rectified by the government or its agent in its place – and that in doing so the government needn't make a loss. Ensuring that liquidity and credit don't evaporate from the financial system is crucial – a function so vital that it can only be carried out by the State or its agents. Labelling the provision of liquidity to a financial

institution in a distressed market a 'bailout' of a private institution is a populist gimmick. It is no different than the case
of a person with a deadly infectious disease, where it is in the
collective interest – as opposed to just social benevolence – for
the government to use taxpayers' money to pay for their hos-
pitalisation and quarantine to prevent the outbreak of a deadly
epidemic. Providing liquidity at a time of severe market stress
and disruption must by definition be made in tenuous circumstances that blur the lines between what is a going concern and
what isn't – as a going concern can go under for the lack of
liquidity. It falls upon the government to provide liquidity in
order to protect taxpayers from the damage of a resulting loss
of confidence and credit crunch. Who else are taxpayers if not
private lenders and borrowers themselves, in effect paying their
government to act in their interests?

Moreover, speed is of the essence. Any hesitation on the
part of the central banks worsens confidence, exacerbates selling
and increases the severity of the economic damage to taxpayers.
Any time lost in getting different government agents to concur
on whether or not a bailout is warranted, in a public show of
deliberation and concern for taxpayers, is counterproductive.

In a similar vein to the Dodd-Frank Act, the Financial
Services Act of 2012 in the UK led to the creation of the Financial
Policy Committee (FPC) at the Bank of England. The FPC is
charged with identifying, monitoring and reducing systemic
risks that may destabilise the financial system. The Act also
created the Prudential Regulation Authority (PRA) to promote
the safety and soundness of banks, building societies, credit
unions, insurers and major investment firms, and to protect
insurance policyholders. As the Bank of England's website states,

'In promoting safety and soundness, the PRA focuses primarily on the harm that firms can cause to the stability of the UK financial system.'[2]

As the central banks set the price of money, act as lenders of last resort and ultimately control money supply, they must naturally be involved in the supervision of the financial system. However, the central banks' actions – well-intentioned as they might be – are a major threat to the economy. By their very nature, systemic risks arise in response to monetary policy. This is the one constant that all economic participants face, and their responses to it can stack up high enough to threaten the economy.

In any trading or banking operation, there is a separation between traders and risk managers, to ensure that there is no conflict of interest between the police (the risk managers who monitor the traders) and those who are being policed (traders who take risks on behalf of their institutions). Not so in the case of the FSOC, FPC and PRA. By including the heads of central banks and members of the rate-setting committees, they are no more than sham councils in which traders double as risk managers. In the current setup taxpayers are therefore not adequately protected against the concentration of power at the central banks and the human error caused by hubris as a result. The consequences are too large and long term for these organisations to continue unchallenged in their current incarnations.

For there to be a meaningful monitoring of any systemic risks, it must be done by an expert body that sits outside the central banks and is tasked with assessing the quality of outcome of monetary policy. It should have the authority to neutralise the impact of monetary policy in the event that short-term gains come at the cost of a build-up of economic fragility that then increases the risk of future crises. Nearly a decade since the beginning of the 2007–09 financial crisis, the central banks are still focused on consumer price inflation, when it was monetary excess that had bypassed the real economy that was the defining feature of the run-up to both the 2007–09 crisis and the Great Depression. Hence, the raison-d'être of such an expert body should be one of being alert to any monetary excess that bypasses the gauge of the price level – to foster economic sustainability and not just financial stability.

The banks didn't go into the financial crisis as freewheeling unregulated entities. In May 2009, Ben Bernanke said:

The Fed has supervisory and regulatory authority over bank holding companies (including financial holding companies), state-chartered banks that choose to join the Federal Reserve System (state member banks), the U.S. operations of foreign banking organisations, and certain types of U.S. entities that engage in international banking. We work with other federal and state supervisory authorities to promote the safety and soundness of the banking industry, foster the stability of the broader financial system, and help ensure fair and equitable treatment of consumers in their financial transactions... During the current crisis, supervisory expertise and information have repeatedly proved invaluable in helping us to address potential systemic risks involving specific financial institutions and markets and to effectively fulfil our role as lender of last resort.[3]

This was testament to the fact that the Fed had comprehensive understanding of the financial system and adequate reach in terms of supervisory authority. The investment banking arms of the commercial banks provided adequate knowledge of the scale of derivatives, nature of securitisation and extent of leverage in the financial system. Moreover, the Federal Reserve's own quarterly statistics provided information on the balance sheet of all sectors of the economy; data that signalled the increase in overall leverage and financial fragility and was flashing red well ahead of time when policy could have changed course to avert crisis. The reason the central banks did not stop the credit build-up in its tracks, or raise the prospect of higher capital levels, was because in loosening lending standards and financial innovation the banking system was simply responding to the instruction of monetary policy – first, explicitly when rates were kept low and then implicitly by the slow pace of rate hikes over a two-year period. There is a risk that proactive provisioning of reserves and negative real interest rates do not ensure ample income streams, and the central banks knowingly took that risk. Only the risk did not collectively pay off; something for which banks and investors have at best diminished responsibility, given the incentives that the loss of purchasing power creates and the implicit claim that low rates are an effective lever to foster sustainable economic growth and stability. If the banks were somehow guilty of foul play, the central banks were at least complicit.

An economic slowdown and falling asset prices inevitably deplete banks' capital and liquidity provisions – hence the more, the better. To this extent, the Basel III reforms proposed by the Basel Committee on Banking Supervision – a body comprised of national banking regulators and central banks – are significant.

The proposed measures aim for greater capital requirements, liquidity provisioning and better capture of leverage, all of which will be made progressively effective from 2013 to 2019. These measures will come to constitute a new international standard. No doubt they will make the banking system more resilient in future.

The game of bluff, however, was never just between central banks and the banking sector. It was more broadly between savers and borrowers. Basel III may indeed make the banking sector more robust, but it still leaves unsolved the problem of asset price fragility, and shifts the focal point of loss directly on to savers. Society as a whole remains vulnerable to asset price declines and the losses that result from misallocation of savings to investments, the true value of which is camouflaged by negative real interest rates and the central banks' arm twisting.

Moreover, even with larger amounts of capital, the banks can never be fully immune to declines in asset prices. Given their frontline position, they will always be the infantry in the line of bluff and will bear the brunt of an economic recession in which asset prices fall disproportionally. They will inevitably become less keen to lend, and will end up amplifying the strife. But for all its amplification, it is important to remember they will not be the ones to have started the war.

Part V

—————

Towards Stability

25

True Liberty

To those who say it was laissez-faire economics and freewheeling banks that brought us the never-ending crutch of low interest rates and asset markets caught up in whirlwinds and downspins – know that it wasn't so. It wasn't laissez-faire but the hubris that denigrated human ingenuity to lethargy that can be tricked, prodded and controlled with an inflation stick.

To those who say 'inflation, what inflation?' – know that you fool only yourselves. As those who could protect themselves from the surfeit of paper money rushed for capital assets, the payoffs of which adjust higher to account for inflation.

To those who say that their hearts bleed for the unemployed – know that low interest rates have done us no favours. It has led to a misallocation of human, physical and financial capital, produced a generation that doesn't know what job security means, and created an income–capital divide that has eroded social cohesion.

To those who say that the central banks have used interest rates to remove the vicissitudes of economic cycles – know that they have done no such thing. All they have done is pump up asset prices, brought spending forward by way of debt, and created a much bigger problem further down the line.

To those who say that every policy has trade-offs, that policies are justified so long as society as a whole is richer and the poorest are just slightly better off – know that your claim is dishonest. When you factor in all the tangible and intangible after-effects of central banks' discretion in setting interest rates, society is actually economically worse off, as the rise in government debt will testify.

To those who say that inflation is justified to free ourselves of debt – know that this easy path has hidden pitfalls. It has doomed us to evaluate debt not in terms of the value it will be used to create, but on the basis of how easily we can reduce its real burden over time. It has created a perverse situation where credit is less likely to be the enabler of enterprise and more likely to stack up as a deadweight burden – one that then needs ever more inflation to do away with it.

To those who say that inequality has increased, and that the rich must be taxed – know that any tax on wealth does little to confiscate the gains acquired by the asset-rich, if monetary policy keeps inflating them disproportionately. Taxing symbols of wealth punishes human diligence and ingenuity that honestly earns its way to wealth, while encouraging governments to create an ever larger surfeit of paper money that they can then tax surreptitiously.

It took two decades of runaway consumer price inflation for the intellectual consensus to concede that it had mistakenly inferred from the correlation between prosperity and inflation that inflation would ensure prosperity. Unfortunately, just as it realised this, the consensus fell for another misbelief: because prosperity led to higher asset wealth, boosting asset prices would generate prosperity. Over the two subsequent decades, this fallacy led us to a mountain of debt, recurring economic crises and greater inequality. It falls upon us now to rid ourselves of the pretence that central banks can smooth economic cycles by boosting asset prices through the interest rate lever.

The lesson gleaned from the Great Depression was that it was important to prevent the price level from falling, as this increased the real burden of debt and affected spending and profits. The wisdom that followed was that policy makers had to prevent prices from dropping below the existing general price level at which debt had been created. In the event that prices did fall, the implication was that they would have to inflate back up to a point at which the general price level was restored. What didn't follow was an excuse to create a perennial loss of purchasing power.

The concept of inflation targeting removed the need for an arbitrary physical constraint in the shape of a limited commodity, which would prevent the central banks from issuing too much paper money. The intellectual basis of inflation targeting was set out as far back as 1898, when Knut Wicksell wrote, 'At any moment and in every economic situation there is a certain level of the average rate of interest which is such that the general level of prices has no tendency to move either upwards or downwards.'[1]

Wicksell asserted that inflationary pressures arise because a limited amount of capital goods is met by potentially unlimited demand created by excess paper money. The supply of real capital goods is itself limited due to the physical constraints of labour, liquid capital, land and productivity that are all needed to produce them. As these capital goods pay rents for eternity and are acquired by credit, a fall in the cost of borrowing (symptomatic of excess paper money) has a disproportionate impact on their prices, which then feeds wider inflation.

If paper money did not exist, the price of capital or the rate of interest would be determined by the natural demand and supply of real capital goods. At this cost of capital, which Wicksell called the natural rate of interest on capital, demand and supply would be in perfect balance. With the existence of paper money, however, the prevailing cost of borrowing can differ from this theoretical natural cost of capital. And this discrepancy causes too much money chasing a limited supply of capital goods, which leads to, in Wicksell's words, a progressive and cumulative rise in prices.

It was on this concept of a natural rate of capital that Milton Friedman based his theory of a natural rate of unemployment. That theory evolved into the more familiar concept of Nairu (non-accelerating inflation rate of unemployment) – the level of unemployment below which inflation starts to rise at an accelerating pace. The implication is that as more people become employed, the fight for labour among employers increases and wages spike at an increasing rate. This wage inflation then translates into the prices of consumer goods and services because people are able to pay more for them.

A natural rate of interest on capital is a harder concept to grasp and lacked the intuitive ease of Nairu, which couches inflationary pressures in a shortage of labour. However, if we just think in terms of accelerating inflation due to a labour shortage, we obscure the fact that capital assets are the primary receptacle

of a surfeit of paper money created by a lower cost of borrowing. And that implicit in any progressive and cumulative or
accelerating rise in the general price level, there is a presumed
translation of capital asset inflation into that of consumer goods
and services.

Wicksell's policy prescription in light of the fact that the
natural rate of interest was not observable was to alter the cost
of borrowing in the marketplace (which was both observable
and controllable), up until the point that the general level of
prices was neither rising nor falling. Though the central banks
currently pretend to do the same, the moment they target a
positive rate of inflation and then set the rate of return below it,
they create expectations of a loss of purchasing power caused by
a surfeit of money. And no sooner have these inflationary expectations been created by the central banks than they get funnelled
into capital assets (without impacting consumer prices) and are
more inclined to stay trapped in them as they offer protection
against a cumulative loss of purchasing power over time. Hence,
for inflation targeting to work as a concept, there must be a genuine commitment to preserving the purchasing power of money.

Central banks should therefore target a general price level
that will be the same in 2015 as it will be in 2115, just as it was
through much of the 100 years preceding the First World War.
A unit of currency would then have the same purchasing power
through time. This would remove the weapon of negative real
interest rates from central banks and dispel the illusion that they
can use them to create short-term boosts in growth to do away
with boom and bust.

Such a policy would remove people's panic that they might
lose their savings to eroding purchasing power, which is the

main incentive for them to chase capital assets, and the reason that unsustainable asset price bubbles develop in the first place. It would greatly lessen the debt that people take on to buy property as an insurance against a surfeit of paper money in the economy. And it would encourage the creation of credit that had a reasonable chance of producing a strong enough income stream – one that paid for itself, even at higher interest rates. Risk-taking would be steered more towards the creation of value, all but insensitive to the central banks' bluff.

Simplifying the central banks' main task list would recognise that they cannot be the superheroes we expect them to be – somehow maximising employment, securing purchasing power and creating a stable financial system at the same time. But by no means would it make their role any less crucial. They would still set interest rates with the aim of securing a stable general price level, one that is neither rising nor falling. The anticipated 2 per cent consumer price inflation rate would fall to zero. The central banks would still have to prevent the general price level from falling, as the Fed let happen during the Great Depression. They would have to ensure that the financial system was stable and able to provide credit at all times, and stand ready to provide the necessary liquidity in the event of a market panic. The likelihood of market panics, though, would itself diminish as credit created by the financial system would naturally be more productive and value-creating.

In the provision of liquidity to the banking sector, the focus of the central banks must naturally be on the quality of assets on the banks' balance sheets. Any banking crisis is firstly the result of misallocation of capital due to the coercive nature of negative real interest rates, then a regulatory failure, and lastly due to misguided risk-taking on the part of commercial and investment bankers. Central bankers should therefore, similar to the commercial and investment bank executives, have their performance-linked pay (or any remuneration that is above the average salary for civil servants) or pensions clawed back if a regulated financial institution later collapses due to insufficient collateral and lack of liquidity. This would go some way towards protecting taxpayers from regulatory and policy errors by the central bankers.

The central banks would still have plenty of discretion over how to achieve their goal of a static general price level and a stable financial system. Ideally, the remuneration of central bankers would be linked to variations in the general price level. As inflation would have to be followed by deflation, which would be uncomfortable for all, there would be little temptation for the central banks to create inflation in the first place. Besides, if they can successfully anchor inflation at 2 per cent, then they can just as well do so at zero.

The question some people would naturally ask is, 'What happens if an unchanging general price level coincides with an economic slowdown? In that event, shouldn't central banks be lowering interest rates to propel growth?' It would be natural for the public to reach this conclusion, as it has been programmed to think that way. There would be a role for central banks to lower interest rates if they could deliver sustainable growth by generating inflation. But the past two decades of wrongly channelled inflationary expectations and booms and busts in asset prices are proof that they can't. The recurring financial crises since the late 1990s were a result of policy errors by the central banks as opposed to the greed and deceit of commercial and investment bankers. No sooner have we realised that, than it becomes apparent that the best they can do is provide price stability in the real sense of unchanging purchasing power.

Going by the Keynesian diagnosis of unemployment and sub-par growth, the answer would be to boost aggregate demand, with the government taking on that responsibility. To fill in for the lack of private enterprise in a recession, there is a natural case for the government to engage in productive and value-creating activity that should prove non-inflationary given unused resources to begin with. Moreover, a boost to consumer spending should come first and foremost from cutting taxes on consumption (sales and value-added tax [VAT]). After all, it does seem absurd that an agent of the government (the central bank) should try to boost aggregate spending by cutting interest rates, when the government itself – as it is in the UK – is dampening spending with a value-added tax on consumption of 20 per cent!

Using the value-added or sales tax as an instrument to boost aggregate demand when the economy enters a slowdown has the great benefit of balanced growth, rather than skewing demand towards capital assets. As producers respond to the increased demand that results from a tax rebate, they will be more inclined to hire and uniformly produce more. Alternatively, to avoid a situation wherein producers choose not to pass on the tax rebate to consumers, the government could allow consumers to seek refunds on any VAT or sales taxes they paid. Any administrative costs this would incur would be worth it because of the feel-good boost to consumers of getting anywhere up to 20 per cent cash back on their spending. This boost would also mean that people would be less likely to save and stumble into the paradox of thrift.

The psychological benefit of knowing that a slowdown means relief from a very onerous tax on consumption, one over and above income taxes, would be tremendous. Moreover, as those on lower incomes – rather than the wealthy – spend more of their income, the effect would be progressive in the sense of being of greater benefit to the less well-off. And because cuts in taxes on consumption mean that consumers needn't become indebted in the first place in order to benefit, the government can pull the economy out of recession without an inadvertent increase in leverage in the private sector.

The setting of interest rates would be no different from the central banks' current *modus operandi*: with a target of zero inflation, in effect the central banks would not be able to inflict negative real interest rates. If the general price level was falling even when the central banks had set their short-term lending rate to zero, they would still have the freedom to ease further via unconventional methods, though only to raise the price level to where it had been (in other words, strictly reflating, not inflating). As for the question of what would constitute a general price level, in essence it would be no different from what we have today – the price level of a general basket of consumer goods and services would suffice.

A zero inflation target would also have to be something that all the main central banks agreed to converge to: otherwise, inflationary currencies would depreciate, seemingly bestowing a competitive advantage to their exporters. However, even if a particular country was the only one to target zero inflation, the benefits gained from long-term stability and real economic growth would likely outweigh any short-term loss due to a fall in exports.

Resistance to committing to a zero inflation rate policy would most likely come from the government itself. It might argue that inflation was the only way to deal with an existing mountain of debt without encumbering future generations. The government wouldn't be alone in thinking this way: all those who had racked up big debts would be relying on inflation to bail them out. The trouble with this argument is precisely where it ends. If today's debt is to be justified by more inflation tomorrow, then how can the public be sure that there isn't another stash of unproductive debt created by this expectation and that yet more loss of purchasing power will be inflicted upon it – over and above the taxation it is already suffering? Inflation, really, is nothing but a form of stealth taxation: one that the government doesn't have to account for. As a middle-ground solution, commitment to a zero inflation policy can be achieved over a period of time. Gradual inflation up to that point may reduce the real burden of existing debt. But in the meantime a change in expectations by itself may limit the imprudent creation of credit any further.

Can the central banks deliver a static general price level, or is this too much to ask? A large part of their ability to deliver on any target, whether it is zero or 2 per cent, depends on how honestly they commit to it. If there were bouts of above-target inflation that were never rectified in the future, inflation targeting would obviously be seen as a sham, highlighted by the resulting differential levels of price inflation for capital assets and consumer goods and services. But other than a lack of will, there is nothing to stop central banks delivering zero inflation within the continuity of the current framework. After all, any anticipated level of inflation is a mere distraction, because all private economic contracts factor it in. A zero inflation policy merely removes the central bank's ability to inflict negative real interest rates. Any hysteria about deflation and depression if inflation edged below zero would be uncalled for: a commitment to a genuinely stable price level would leave the public reassured that any edging below would soon be rectified, just as any slippage above the zero rate would also be corrected.

Though a policy of zero inflation will remove a major psychological cause of asset price bubbles, it is fair to say that human nature can never be completely immune from getting suckered into get-rich-quick schemes and herding into imprudent investments. But as history bears witness, this behaviour is likely to be sporadic, and might only afflict a generation every now and then, if at all. As long as the banks are well capitalised and supervised, the negative impact of any such unsustainable, exaggerated shifts will be localised. What would become a thing of the past would be the mass psychosis in equity, real estate and debt markets that has been systematically created by central banks on the pretext of managing economic growth. No longer would an agent of the State be aiding and abetting a latent inclination in human nature to make extravagant extrapolations about potential asset price gains.

26

The Uncertainty Principle

In 1927, Werner Heisenberg put forth the uncertainty principle of quantum mechanics in a departure from classical
physics that 'presupposes that exact simultaneous values
can be assigned to all physical quantities'.[1] He countered this
presumption by illustrating that it wasn't possible to measure the
position and momentum of sub-atomic particles simultaneously
with equal accuracy. The accuracy with which the position of
an electron can be measured depends on the wavelength of the
light used to illuminate it. To increase this accuracy, we must use
light of shorter wavelength. However, in so doing, the interaction
between the electron and the illuminating light itself cannot
be ignored. It so happens that the collision between the light
photon and the electron disturbs the latter's momentum – the
shorter the wavelength of the illuminating light, the greater is
the disturbance to the momentum. The uncertainty principle
therefore states that the more precisely we measure the position
of an electron, the less precisely we can gauge its momentum;
and vice versa. To put it another way – the more certain we are
about one aspect, the less certain we can be about the other.

We can think of the quantity and quality of credit created in an economy as being subject to the same trade-off. The more certain we are about the quantity of credit that is created by lowering interest rates, the less certain we can be of its quality (as defined by the probability of default by the borrower). This is because a low interest rate shifts the focus from the robustness and durability of the income stream that is generated from an investment on to affordability by virtue of a lower debt service cost. As more debt becomes affordable, more credit is created. However, just because more credit is created does not necessarily increase the stream of future income that will eventually pay for the higher amount of credit creation. For instance, a borrower can borrow $600,000 at 5 per cent per year or $1.5 million at 2 per cent per year – the yearly interest cost in both cases is $30,000. So as the debt service cost is the same, a lower cost of borrowing allows for a greater amount of borrowing. The rental income that results from, say, a property financed by increased borrowing permitted by a lower interest rate may, however, remain the same in the future or decrease and there may not be further appreciation in its value, even though the amount of debt that needs to be paid off has increased. At best therefore there is an increased amount of uncertainty about return of principal that is associated with a higher amount of credit that is created.

In the retribution that followed the financial crisis of 2007–09, the clawback of bankers' bonuses is supposedly a way of ensuring both quantity and quality of credit created in response to a low rate policy. In a free market system, however, economic activity is driven by prices, which trump all subjective evaluation. Moreover, the entire purpose of lowering rates in the first place is to send a price signal of cheaper money to make what was previously unaffordable affordable in order to encourage greater risk-taking at a collective level. Bankers are, however, expected to circumvent the all-powerful signal of prices that is engineered by the central banks and exercise a very strong value judgement about who to extend credit to, in the pretence that in so doing, they can alter the increased uncertainty inherent in greater risk-taking.

Imagine that the government has just mandated that all chocolate is to be sold at a penny a bar, but that supermarkets must decide who to sell it to. Supermarkets will be held responsible for any increase in obesity and diabetes that occurs as a result of this near-free chocolate. Consequently, all supermarkets must exercise a value judgement at the moment of sale to determine if buyers have a predisposition for obesity, diabetes, general indolence and gluttony. That seems an unreasonable responsibility to place on supermarkets when in altering the price of chocolate the intention is to increase its consumption by the wider population and that a higher risk of disease follows as a consequence. Likewise the burden of longer-term economic repercussions is unfairly pinned on commercial and investment bankers, who are merely responding to the price signal of cheaper rates as intended and cannot be held responsible for the greater uncertainty associated with an increase in credit, particularly when it is at a collective level. This is especially true when central banks goad them into lowering their criteria in the event that they choose to be selective.

The central banks feel justified in their actions amidst joblessness – they presume that the debt being created will lead to jobs and higher incomes, even though the uncertainty principle is just as valid regardless of the extent of unemployment in the economy. Greater credit creation when more people are unemployed does not guarantee that the nature of investments that are financed are necessarily of a robust nature. Just as lowering the price of chocolate when people are hungry does not mean that it is necessarily good for them, or that it will provide the nutrition they require.

As part of an attempt by governments to ensure financial stability, central banks were given the added responsibility of dictating extra loss-absorbing capital requirements to banks during an economic boom (hence, counter to what good economic times call for), in preparation for an ensuing bust. The intention is also to slow down credit being supplied by the banking sector when high interest rates do not prove an adequate curb to credit growth. The implication that bad credit is created in the last stages of an economic boom blurs the fact once again that a trade-off between the quality and quantity of credit exists at all times. Increased indebtedness that results from low interest rates comes with increased uncertainty of repayment, irrespective of when in the economic cycle it is created.

A greater loss-absorbing capital cushion may make the banks more resilient, but it does not rectify the error in the first place: that cheap money accompanied by a loss of purchasing power under the pretext of boosting confidence and unleashing animal spirits[2] incentivises economic players to increase leverage and chase capital assets.

If debt is a contractual obligation between lender (bank) and borrower (householder/corporate), then by definition the process of securitisation that effectively parcels out this contractual obligation as investment securities implies that demand is coming from third-party investors outside the banking sector – from pension funds, institutional and private savings. In response to a surfeit of cheap money, these savers bought securitised assets and associated derivatives in the run-up to the US housing market collapse that precipitated the 2007–09 crisis. To use our previous example, in so doing they were effectively lending $1.5 million as opposed to $600,000 to earn the same return of $30,000 per year. Greater leverage to earn the same amount of return in response to monetary policy came with greater risk of wealth destruction. The problem was compounded because the brokers that package and sell these securities – namely, the investment banks – held on to some of these assets and sustained losses that threatened the rest of the banking sector. Had they acted just as brokers, the banks would have taken less of a direct hit, and this, coupled with more capital to absorb losses from a collapse in asset prices, would have made for a more resilient banking system. However, irrespective of the 'who and what' specifics of excessive risk-taking, the inherent trade-off between quantity and quality in response to negative real interest rates will always exist.

The focus needs to shift from financial stability that requires a more resilient banking sector to a wider concept of economic stability – one that favours quality over quantity and minimises the destruction of wealth due to misallocation of resources. If money were to hold its purchasing power, there would be no urgent need to chase risky investments without adequately evaluating the robustness of the potential income stream. This in turn would lead to less misallocation of capital, a greater probability of value creation and less chance of wealth destruction due to a collapse in asset prices. The by-product of this economic and price stability would be a stronger banking sector and a more long-term value-creating and robust economy – one not intermittently plagued by large, adverse shifts in asset prices.

27

Economics and Ideology

In the guilt and blame that followed the financial debacle of 2007–09, economics suffered the accusation of being a wannabe science that had lost its relevance. Perhaps predictably amidst a severe economic upheaval, we would expect the pummelling of a subject that claims to explain the laws that govern the production and distribution of income and wealth. If, however, we are to judge the strength of a subject by its internal consistency and its breadth, then economics lies untainted. Its relevance is little diminished since the crisis, because sustaining and maximising income and wealth remain as important as ever.

Unfortunately, by its nature economics is very susceptible to ideology – a forceful subset of knowledge that attempts to silence competing thoughts and bestride social consciousness based on a presumed and good-intentioned superiority. The belief that negative real interest rates and the slow bleed of purchasing power that they inflict are the key to forcing the public to achieve its economic potential is mere ideology. And like all ideologies, it has embedded itself in social consciousness by exploiting a fear that the conditions of the Great Depression may be re-created.

Given inflation's association with prosperity, the notion that it was inherently a good thing was hard to shake off. This was especially true if the bad part – the confusion that results from public expectations of yet more inflation – could be contained. An independent central bank committed to maintaining a low rate of inflation was just what was needed to reassure the public that money would not lose its value by any more than about 2 per cent per year, a rate that people could correctly anticipate and factor in.

If that was what it was – a duff rate of inflation that could be perfectly anticipated and compensated for – then the public had truly won itself respite from the inclination of governments to create inflation. Unfortunately, the 2 per cent rate of inflation was destined as a stealth weapon of negative real interest rates on the pretext of creating employment. It resulted in punitive doses of an effective loss of purchasing power engineered and intended by the central banks as precursors to real growth via the asset price mechanism. But then there was inadequate translation of capital asset price inflation into that of consumer goods and services and this left exaggerated moves in asset prices unsupported by economic reality. The inconvenient result of these asset price bubbles that were destined to burst at some stage had to be reasoned away somehow.

The interplay between finance and economics led to a great deal of literature that focused on the behavioural aspects of investors. It dwelled on how excessive confidence and over-optimism were basic human traits that lent themselves to asset price bubbles. But while this literature focused on how traders and investors were inclined to push up asset prices into bubble territory, it strangely absolved the central bankers of these same supposedly human traits. To err in one's decision-making was something that appeared to affect the people who engaged in trading and investing – but somehow not the men and women who set the price of money to pump up asset values.

The academic literature of the past two decades acknowledges the role of interest rates in the economy only in so far as they are a precursor to growth and consumer price inflation. It falls a long way short of linking low rates to exaggerated gains in the stock market and real estate prices, or to the level of indebtedness in society. Several economists[1] argue that central banks should react to misalignments in asset prices – in effect, curbing excessive investor appetite with higher interest rates to prevent the economic upheaval associated with an eventual bust. However, the reason why this argumentation is ignored by the Jackson Hole consensus is because it naïvely overlooks the fact that asset prices are conduits for growth. And that they are systematically inflated by lower interest rates under the pretext of capital formation and the unleashing of animal spirits – in the hope that they may ultimately become self-sustaining channels. In the event that they did not become self-sustaining because incomes did not follow suit, the central banks would look extremely foolish if they then raised rates to burst what they had painstakingly inflated.

Somewhat lacking in the academic literature is the conviction that asset bubbles are altogether a bad thing. There is a notion[2] that because assets act as conduits of the intergenerational transfer of wealth, they allow older generations to consume more by selling their overpriced, potentially worthless assets to the young. The existence of overvalued assets or bubbles therefore rectifies the problem of too much saving by the young by in effect getting them to fund greater consumption by the old by overpaying for assets held by them. Bursting a bubble, then, means depriving the old of greater consumption in favour of too much saving, even if it is more productively utilised. The conclusion that logically follows is that if an asset bubble bursts of its own accord, policy makers should then create another one. Moreover, as it is more politically astute for policy makers to be focused more on the 'present', they are naturally inclined to favour a policy that allows for 'more consumption now' even if that results in misallocation of capital. Pronounced support for financial markets, which started with Alan Greenspan – but which in no way was limited to him or the Fed – effectively subscribes to this theory. As policy makers generally tend to be older, it seems no coincidence that they effectively endorse a policy that favours older generations.

A line of thinking[3] that exists in academic literature and has never been completely dispelled as a rational explanation for asset bubbles, given its populist appeal, pins the blame on the asset management industry – more specifically, on the compensation structure for fund managers who manage money on behalf of savers. The idea was that there were good and bad fund managers: good fund managers knew how to differentiate between undervalued and overvalued stocks, while the bad ones did not. Savers, however, would not know how to distinguish between good and bad ones – the fact that good fund managers did exist made the whole fund management industry viable. However, it also provided a cover for the bad ones. As fund managers were rewarded for gains but did not share in any losses, what followed was undue risk-taking by bad fund managers who played fast and loose with savers' money, and were therefore willing to pay more for a stock than it was worth. As these bad fund managers were under pressure to produce high returns, they were induced to take more risk by buying overvalued securities, hoping that they could pass these on, in time. In so doing, they helped create a bubble.

This point of view is similar to Keynes's enterprise versus speculation rationale. Good portfolio managers were investing on the basis of long-term income prospects, while bad ones were speculating on what others were thinking, and factoring in the probability and ease with which they could pass off a stock before its price crashed. Because the bad fund managers – spurred on by their bonuses – were willing to pay more for a stock than it was worth, they were inherently to blame for the unsustainable bubbles that emerged and burst.

Pinning the blame for asset price bubbles on traders and the fund management industry might seem convenient. But it ignores the inescapable trends in money management from the 1990s onwards. There are essentially three types of fund managers. Firstly, there is the traditional money manager who takes small risks against a predetermined benchmark like the S&P 500 index or the FTSE all-share index. On the opposite side of the spectrum is the hedge fund manager, who invests independently of any predetermined index. Thirdly, there are those who manage exchange-traded funds or index trackers, which require them simply to replicate an index, allowing investors to gain exposure to the stock market or any other asset class as a whole. Buying an index tracker enables savers to skip an active portfolio manager and avoid undue risk-taking by them in the hope of earning a cut of the gains.

The hedge funds that stood to earn as much as 20 per cent of the returns they made for investors were more interested in selling overvalued stocks or assets in general than in buying them. How their activities can fuel an asset market bubble is unclear. Traditional asset managers who took small risks against a predetermined benchmark could still have been accused of overpaying for assets in lust of a bonus. However, the design of their product meant that, for the most part, fund managers had little choice but to stay fully exposed to the underlying asset class. In doing so, they were acting as nothing more than smart custodians of money which had been directed by savers.

Moreover, through the 1990s the trend was for savers to take their money away from traditional asset managers and reallocate it to hedge funds and exchange-traded trackers instead. The choice of asset class was dictated by savers, and where it was not – as in the case of hedge funds – fund managers were just as incentivised to speculate against overvalued assets as to chase them. Pinning asset bubbles on undue risk-taking by those managing money for savers overlooks the disproportionate impact of interest rates on capital assets and how and why capital allocation decisions are really made.

While people will continue to look elsewhere for reasons why asset price bubbles emerge, the central banks will continue their methods bolstered by an ideology that has lost its efficacy. They are unlikely to admit to bearing chief responsibility for the financial crisis of 2007–09 or to own up to the fact that these exaggerated moves in asset prices were not bubbles as such but 'policy in action' that actually misfired. But sooner or later, the patterns of recurring asset price collapse and unintended consequences will point more firmly in their direction. And it is only to be expected that finger-pointing at the commercial and investment banks will be sharpest and their cries of denial will be loudest just before the strength of public opinion forces change.

28

Endgame

'Wolf! Wolf!' cried the boy, and the villagers came rushing with guns and sticks to ward off the predator and protect the sheep. In Aesop's fable, no wolf actually appears: the boy calls out as a prank as he sits on the hillside watching his sheep. When the villagers arrive, he pretends the wolf has run off, and the villagers commend him for his bravery. A few days later, the boy repeats the prank, and once again out come the villagers to protect the flock. However, on finding no wolf this time either, they become suspicious. A week later, the wolf turns up. As he savages the sheep, the boy cries for help again, but the villagers – thinking he's lying – stay at home. The moral of the story is that you can fool people only once or twice, but you do so at your peril, because they are less likely to fall for the trick next time around.

Lowering interest rates to pump up stock and real estate markets only works if you can make the public simultaneously believe that the economy will recover enough to deliver jobs with requisitely high wages and sufficient earnings for companies. Each time the central banks lower interest rates and cry 'Jobs!

Jobs!', as if they expect wages to follow suit, they leave equity and house prices vulnerable to higher interest rates if adequate wages don't materialise. After each crash, investors lose a little more trust, and become a little less pliable. When global equity markets crashed in 2000, investors believed the central bankers' cries and directed money into real estate. When the markets crashed after Lehman Brothers went under in September 2008, investors were more reluctant to act at first, but were eventually persuaded by an inordinate amount of monetary easing by the central banks. But if interest rates go up yet again and wages and corporate earnings are not enough to sustain the higher asset prices, they may well crash once more. Sooner or later, investors will stop believing the central banks, even when they should.

Such a scenario would be a deflationary collapse triggered by a significant fall in the stock or real estate markets – or both – that dents savings and leaves homeowners in negative equity. At such time, even if central banks lowered interest rates, private creditors and investors would still hesitate to make loans and risky investments. All those who thought they would buy with both hands if there was a market correction would instead find themselves holding back, following a dramatic shift in the collective psychology towards caution. Dented savings and negative equity would make householders retrench, and as they cut back on their spending, businesses would in turn suffer. No matter how good their loss-absorbing capacity, banks would almost certainly restrict credit in the event of falling prices, late payments and business failures. If central banks attempt to engineer further monetary easing by buying more government bonds and other assets from the public, they might find that such action has none of the beneficial impacts it had on previous occasions.

Like the boy who cried wolf once too often, the central banks may discover how a jaded and sceptical public does not fall for their bluff, rendering them powerless as the markets spiral out of control.

Unsurprisingly, this is an outcome that the central banks fear. They also know that they are caught between a rock and a hard place: letting an asset bubble develop as a result of their policy of cheap money, or bursting it before wages can catch up. The recovery following the 2007–09 crisis will therefore be a balancing act. Central banks will try to inflate equity and real estate markets yet want them to stay relatively contained (at least, that's the hope), so that wages can catch up to justify higher prices, independently of interest rates. As the economic crisis was centred on US house prices, the Federal Reserve will be conscious of funnelling cheap money into equity markets – even if it knows that when it comes to stimulating economic activity, it is the easier asset class to use. The central banks would be equally cautious about letting interest rates on government bonds fall to a very low level, because this might signal low confidence about future economic prospects – or, at the other extreme, encourage excessive leverage. So they may well try to talk down asset prices and engineer mini-tremors in the financial markets.

In May 2013, Ben Bernanke somewhat purposely made comments that were seen to contrast with the Fed's official policy of carefully engineered cheap money. This led to significant losses for holders of US Treasury debt, even though it was clear that the US economy was not in a position to withstand higher interest rates. And as interest rates moved abruptly higher, equity markets also fell sharply. The Fed's attempts to talk down markets, however, are unlikely to have a lasting impact. Given the bluff the central banks are trying to pull off, such comments can never be too much of a reality check. Ultimately, the move to higher interest rates in 2013 proved temporary, as rates came back down in line with what the Fed and the Bank of England had stated: that they wouldn't raise them. Equity and real estate markets responded to the renewed reality of low interest rates by surging up yet again.

The 'talk-down' ploy's sole purpose is to stall asset prices and allow for wages to catch up, if by no other means than by gradual inflation. As a strategy to temper their intended conduits while buying time for wages to catch up, it may appear messy and counterproductive. But it is not altogether ineffective. As long as the central banks can eventually contain any market tremors, and do not inadvertently expose any self-created fragility in the process, this is perhaps their only hope of extricating themselves from culpability for two decades of severe financial instability.

It may turn out that the central banks get lucky: their strategy works and they are somehow able to scrape together an elegant enough exit from the low interest rate environment that has been necessary since the 2007–09 crisis. This outcome would be a mix of growth and steady inflation that leads to higher wages and buoyant company earnings, with marginally higher interest rates and lagging asset prices.

However, the premise that the central banks can create growth by manipulating financial markets with yet another dose of cheap money and systematic loss of purchasing power, and that they can curtail higher inflation if need be with higher interest rates, is not without significant cost to the public. The latter risks the medicine of higher interest rates that will inevitably lead to an economic recession. The former risks diverging consumer and asset price appreciation, leading to unsustainable asset booms and eventual bust. Ultimately, the divergent paths of consumer and asset price appreciation risk causing social tensions and economic confusion; chaos with no prior pattern. Ideally, for the central banks' task list to change, they would have to concede that the most they can contribute to growth and stability is to ensure that money has constant purchasing power, while also acting as liquidity providers to the financial system in times of distress. If not, then it is only a matter of time before their bluff fails yet again, leading to another damaging episode of economic volatility.

Progress depends on human ingenuity – ingenuity that is independent of the prod of inflation, which central banks mistakenly believe propels economic growth sustainably. Pumping up house prices and equity markets, and encouraging excessive debt that is likely to sour, is no road to growth. The belief that the central banks can liberate us from economic ups and downs by calibrating interest rates to create growth is wishful thinking. At best they can take credit for cleaning up a mess they created – but not without cost.

Buying already over-inflated assets neither shields people from further inflation nor acts as a prudent pension scheme. People who buy property in the hope of passing it on to their children must know that the best they can do for their kids is to fortify them with courage, the ethic of hard work and the resilience to recover from setbacks. The prices of flats in London may be caught in their own updraught, but for them to continue spiralling higher requires the Bank of England to continue its surfeit of money that then bypasses the real economy, creating the semblance of stability as consumer prices stay relatively muted. That may work for now. But without doubt it is a path that ends in peril.

We are far better off questioning the central banks today, and demanding that our governments promise an unchanging general price level so that the purchasing power of our incomes and savings is not eroded over time. Inflicting negative real interest rates in the name of growth is just as counterproductive as war in the name of peace. It is degradation posing as liberty – an inherent contradiction that scuppers any belief that we can get wealthy by cheating the public of its purchasing power.

Notes

Unless otherwise stated, all economic and markets data is sourced from Bloomberg.

The Need to Question

1 J.S. Mill, *On Liberty* (Norwalk, CT: The Easton Press, 1991), p. 34.
2 Refers generically to deposit-taking institutions.
3 Strictly speaking, sales and purchases of eligible securities on the open market also have a similar effect to discounting. This is explained further in Ch. 3.
4 Technically, the correct term is rediscounting as the price of a debt security is already the discounted value of fixed, future payments.

The Motive for the Bluff

1 The Free Dictionary, available at www.thefreedictionary.com provided by Farlex. (Accessed 15 April 2014.)

From Mere Mortal to Supreme Being

1 The early history of the Bank of England draws upon A. Andreades, *History of the Bank of England* (London: P.S. King and Son, 1909) and R.G. Hawtrey, *A Century of Bank Rate* (London: Longmans, Green & Co. Ltd, 1938).
2 As bills of exchange were no more than letters among trading merchants that acted as a promise to pay on a certain date, they could be converted into

money by discounting the future payment by the interest due between then and now.

3   Office for National Statistics, Long-term indicator of prices of consumer goods and services: 1800 to 2015: Jan 1974 = 100.

4   W. Bagehot, *Lombard Street: A Description of the Money Market* (London: Henry S. King, 1873), Ch. 7. Available at http://oll.libertyfund.org/titles/128. (Accessed 15 October 2015.)

5   Office for National Statistics, Long-term indicator of prices of consumer goods and services: 1800 to 2015: Jan 1974 = 100. For reference, the same index at the end of 1997 stood at 621.3 and at the end of 2014 at 1,010.

6   'According to the calculations of Sir Josiah Stamp, the level of real incomes in Great Britain in the years before the war was four times as great as in the Napoleonic period', L. Robbins, *The Great Depression* (Freeport, NY: Books for Libraries Press, 1971, first published 1934), p. 2. Available at https://mises.org/library/great-depression-0. (Accessed 15 October 2015.)

7   Office for National Statistics, Long-term indicator of prices of consumer goods and services: 1800 to 2015: Jan 1974 = 100.

8   M. Friedman and A.J. Schwartz, *A Monetary History of the United States, 1867–1960* (Princeton, NJ: Princeton University Press, 1993), p. 206, Table 10.

9   Ibid. p. 239.

10 Annual report, Federal Reserve Board, 1923, p. 31. The annual reports are available at https://fraser.stlouisfed.org/title/117.

11 The Federal Reserve System consists of a seven-member Board of Governors and twelve Reserve Banks located in major US cities. While in the early years there was a power struggle between them, by the late 1930s the power to set policy was centralised in the Board while the reserve banks became mechanical, executional arms of the system.

12 Annual report, Federal Reserve Board, 1923, p. 33.

13 Annual report, Federal Reserve Board, 1925, p. 1.

14 A.C. Miller, member of the Federal Reserve Board, before the Senate Committee on Banking and Currency, as quoted by L. Robbins, *The Great Depression*, p. 53.

15 L. Robbins, *The Great Depression*, p. 54.

16 Ibid.

17 Gross domestic product refers to the value of goods and services produced by

labour and property located in a country during a period of time, usually yearly or quarterly. 'Nominal' refers to the value in current prices while 'real' strips away the effect of changes in prices.

18 Annual report, Federal Reserve Board, 1933, pp. 20–21.

19 M. Friedman and A.J. Schwartz, *A Monetary History of the United States, 1867–1960*, p. 327.

20 The yield on a debt obligation/security moves inversely to its price. Consider the following simplified example for illustration. Say, the government promises to pay you $150 in a years' time in exchange for your $100 now. The yield or rate of return, or quite simply the rate of interest, is therefore 50%. However, imagine that soon after someone else thinks it so good a deal to be assured $150 in a years' time that he is ready to pay $120 for the same 'promise to pay' or 'I owe you' from the government. However, no sooner has he paid $120, the return is no longer 50% but drops to 25%. Hence, as the price of a debt obligation goes up, the yield comes down and vice versa.

21 Annual report, Federal Reserve Board, 1951, p. 4.

22 Annual report, Federal Reserve Board, 1979, p. 3.

23 The retail price index measures the changing cost of a fixed basket of goods and services over time similar to the consumer price index, in place since 1996. Differences in formula and coverage of goods and services exist.

24 Bank of England Act 1998, www.legislation.gov.uk.

The *Kung Fu Panda* Effect

1 Where applicable, figures have been rounded up/down for neatness.

2 In the UK, there is no legal reserve requirement. The commercial banks nonetheless maintain current accounts at the Bank of England in order to borrow funds to meet any liquidity needs.

3 Subject to other liquidity and capital requirements as well.

A Medicinal Dose of Inflation

1 In January 2012, the Federal Open Market Committee announced an explicit target of 2% as a longer-run goal for inflation, as measured by the annual change in the price index for personal consumption expenditures. Prior to this date, the commitment to target the rate of inflation was an implicit one.

2 K. Wicksell, *Geldzins und Guterpreise / Interest and Prices: A Study of the Causes Regulating the Value of Money* (Jena: Gustav Fischer, 1898, trans. R.F. Kahn), p. 3.
3 Ibid.

The Jewel in the Crown

1 The government is considered to be a risk-free borrower, because its ability to pay is backed by its power to tax the public, and because it, or the central bank as its agent, can create money if need be. Therefore, the holder is assured of return of principal and interest. Of course, however, there is always a risk of high inflation, which means that although savers would still receive their principal and interest payments back from the government, the real purchasing power of their money would be markedly less, making their investments not quite risk-free in the truest sense.

2 Government debt securities are issued for various terms or times to maturity, from the very short term to ten years and beyond. 'Bond' is usually used to refer to debt securities with a longer term, more than ten years. For instance, a debt security issued by the US Treasury that has a maturity of ten years is referred to as a Treasury note, whereas a Treasury bond has a term to maturity of greater than ten years. Debt securities issued by the UK government are generically referred to as gilts, which are differentiated as short-, medium- and long-term gilts. It is nonetheless common to refer to all debt securities that pay a fixed income or interest as bonds. When 'bond' is used here in the more colloquial sense, its maturity is stated to avoid confusion.

3 The present value of an infinite constant stream of income can be calculated as the sum of an infinite geometric series, which effectively is the annual pay-out divided by the long-term cost of borrowing.

4 This is the formula for present value of an infinite, constant stream of income as in the real estate example. More intuitively, think of it as a rate of return. You've paid $20 for owning a share in a company that pays $1 yearly as income. Therefore, the return on your initial investment is 5% per year (1 ÷ 20).

5 For purposes of clarity, the term yield (yield to maturity) is used interchangeably with rate of return and rate of interest on a debt security.

6 1 divided by 0.08 to reflect the fact that the risk-free yield has fallen from 5% to 4% but the risk premium still stays at 4%.

260

7   1 divided by 0.06 to reflect the fact that the risk-free yield has fallen from 5% to 4% and the risk premium has fallen from 4% to 2%.

8   Under normal economic conditions, when government bond yields are not manipulated by the central bank, the ten-year risk-free yield should at least compensate for inflation and the real rate of growth (over and above inflation) at which the economy grows. The latter represents the opportunity cost of lending to the government that the investor may derive from investing elsewhere in the economy. In other words, the ten-year risk-free yield should at least be equal to the prevailing actual/nominal growth rate of the economy, which equals real growth plus inflation.

9   Matthew 8:13, King James Version: 'Go thy way; and as thou hast believed, *so* be it done unto thee.'

The Watchdog

1   Using the previous example as an illustration of the overall market: an initial rent of $10,000 per annum and a mortgage rate of 6% gives a valuation of $166, 666 as $10,000 ÷ 6% = $166,666. A 10% fall in net rent leads to a value of $180,000 if the cost of borrowing, i.e. the mortgage rate, falls to 5% as $9,000 ÷ 5% = $180,000. We therefore arrive at an 8% rise in property price as $180,000 is 8% higher than $166,666.

2   A 5% increase in rents of $9,000 per year gives us a figure of $9,450, which combined with a 4% mortgage rate results in a value of $236,250, which is 31% higher than $180,000.

3   In our example, rents rise a further 20% to $11,340. With mortgage rates at 4.5%, this gives a value of $252,000, which is 51% higher than the initial level of $166,666.

The Jackson Hole Consensus

1   Dividends are not included in all mention of price moves in equity markets.

2   B. Bernanke and M. Gertler, 'Monetary Policy and Asset Price Volatility: Proceedings – Economic Policy Symposium' (Jackson Hole, WY: Federal Reserve Bank of Kansas City, 1999).

Intention Versus Incentives

1 The Upanishads, Brihadaranyaka IV 4.5, introduced and translated by Eknath Easwaran (Berkeley, CA: Nilgiri Press, Blue Mountain Center of Meditation, 1987, 2007).
2 K. Wicksell, *Interest and Prices*, p. 96.
3 Ibid.
4 Ibid.

Speculation Versus Enterprise

1 J.M. Keynes, *The General Theory of Employment, Interest, and Money* (Norwalk, CT: The Easton Press, 1995, first published 1936), p. 159.
2 Ibid.

The Fed's Reflation Prescription in the 1990s

1 Household disposable income is broadly comprised of labour earnings; earnings from ownership of capital assets: rents, interest and dividends; and any net government handouts received less taxes. 'Wages' is used interchangeably with 'labour earnings', to refer to compensation earned by employees as well as proprietors' income that accrues to self-owned businesses/self-employed.
2 In the fourth quarter of 1993, nominal GDP grew at 7.7%, quarter on quarter, seasonally adjusted annualised rate. All GDP growth rates are stated in nominal terms that include the effects of inflation, unless otherwise stated to be in real terms.
3 S&P/Case-Shiller US National Home Price Index.
4 Extracted from household disposable income. It includes compensation of employees and proprietors' income with inventory valuation and capital consumption.
5 The Federal Reserve Board, remarks by chairman Alan Greenspan, at the Annual Dinner and Francis Boyer Lecture of The American Enterprise Institute for Public Policy Research, Washington DC, 5 December 1996.
6 Quarter on quarter, seasonally adjusted annualised rate.

Reflation Redux

1 S&P/Case-Shiller US National Home Price Index.
2 Financial Accounts of the United States (Z.1), Board of Governors of the Federal Reserve System.
3 Ibid.
4 Between March 2004 and June 2006.
5 Excluding food and energy from the basket of consumer goods and services.

John's House

1 Household disposable income.
2 Bank of England, Minutes of Monetary Policy Committee Meeting, 7 and 8 October 1998, p. 6.
3 Data produced by Land Registry Crown Copyright 2015.
4 England and Wales account for 90% of the UK's household disposable income.
5 Bank of England, Minutes of Monetary Policy Committee Meeting, 1 and 2 August 2001, p. 9.
6 Labour earnings extracted out of household disposable income. They include compensation of employees (wages and salaries and employer social contributions) and gross operating surplus and gross mixed income. Source: Office for National Statistics, United Kingdom Economic Accounts, household and non-profit institutions serving households.

A Dark Shadow

1 For tax year 6 April 2015 to 5 April 2016, higher rate of 40% applies to £31,786 to £150,000. People with the standard Personal Allowance start paying this rate on income over £42,385. Source: HMRC.
2 As of January 2016, Land Registry, all figures rounded.

Under the Hood

1 Interest of $48 million is deducted out of $600 million, so it amounts to $552 million. But as 24 million shares have been bought back, the $552 million in earnings are divided only by 76 million shares outstanding to arrive at $7 per share in earnings.

2   Financial Accounts of the United States (Z.1), Board of Governors of the Federal
    Reserve System.

The Bubble That Never Burst

1   Data produced by Land Registry Crown Copyright 2015.
2   Source: Government of Japan, Ministry of Land, Infrastructure and Transport.
3   S&P/Case-Shiller Composite of home prices in Boston, Chicago, Denver, Las
    Vegas, Los Angeles, Miami, New York City, San Diego, San Francisco and
    Washington DC.
4   Regional Gross Disposable Household Income (GDHI) published on 4 June 2014.
    Regional Accounts, Office for National Statistics.
5   Department of Communities and Local Government, Table 577. (Accessed 15
    October 2015.)
6   For the nineteen boroughs of outer London median house prices to median earnings
    stood at 9.1 in 2013. The statistics use gross earnings of full-time employees.
7   Assume that people pay 20% in income tax, so earnings after tax = 0.8 × gross
    annual earnings. If people pay 25% of their net of tax earnings in rent, then annual
    rent = 0.25 × 0.8 × gross annual earnings. If house price/gross annual earnings
    = 10.4, then the number of years needed to pay off the purchase price or house
    price/annual rent = 10.4 ÷ (0.25 × 0.8) = 52 years.
8   Assume that people pay 20% in income tax, so earnings after tax = 0.8 × gross
    annual earnings. If people pay 20% of their net of tax earnings in rent, then annual
    rent = 0.2 × 0.8 × gross annual earnings. If house price/gross annual earnings =
    6.72, then the number of years needed to pay off the purchase price or house price/
    annual rent = 6.72 ÷ (0.2 × 0.8) = 42 years.

Infantry in the Line of Bluff

1   www.banking.senate.gov/public/_files/070110_Dodd_Frank_Wall_Street_Reform_
    comprehensive_summary_Final.pdf. (Accessed 31 October 2015.) Also available at
    http://democrats.financialservices.house.gov/uploadedfiles/media/file/key_issues/
    financial_regulatory_reform/comprehensive_summary_finalv5.pdf.
2   http://www.bankofengland.co.uk/pra/Pages/publications/prafoi.aspx. (Accessed
    15 January 2016.)

3   Chairman Ben S. Bernanke, 'Lessons of the Financial Crisis for Banking Supervision', at the Federal Reserve Bank of Chicago Conference on Bank Structure and Competition, Chicago (via satellite), 7 May 2009.

True Liberty

1   K. Wicksell, *Interest and Prices*, p. 120.

The Uncertainty Principle

1   J. Hilgevoord and J. Uffink, 'The Uncertainty Principle', *The Stanford Encyclopaedia of Philosophy (Spring 2014 Edition)*, ed. Edward N. Zalta, http://plato.stanford. edu/archives/spring 2014/entries/qt-uncertainty/

2   Phrase used by Keynes to describe the emotive quality of the spontaneity that propels human beings into action. J.M. Keynes, *The General Theory of Employment, Interest, and Money*, p. 161.

Economics and Ideology

1   S.G. Cechetti, H. Genberg and S. Wadhwani, 'Asset Prices in a Flexible Inflation Targeting Framework' (2002). Prepared for the conference on 'Asset Price Bubbles; Implications for Monetary, Regulatory and International Policies' organised jointly by the Federal Reserve Bank of Chicago and the World Bank, Chicago, 22–24 April 2002. (This view is, however, not limited to the authors of this paper.)

2   See the following paper for a description of viewpoints on socially desirable bubbles: G. Barlevy, 'Rethinking Theoretical Models of Bubbles', in *New Perspectives on Asset Price Bubbles*, ed. D.D. Evanoff, G.G. Kaufman and A.G. Malliaris (Oxford: Oxford University Press, 2012).

3   F. Allen and G. Gorton, 'Churning Bubbles' (1993), in *New Perspectives on Asset Price Bubbles* (2012).

Index

References to notes are indicated by n.

267

Index